A PAUPER'S HISTORY OF ENGLAND

A PAUPER'S HISTORY OF ENGLAND

1,000 Years of Peasants, Beggars and Guttersnipes

Peter Stubley

PEN & SWORD
HISTORY

First published in Great Britain in 2015 by
PEN AND SWORD HISTORY
an imprint of
Pen and Sword Books Ltd
47 Church Street
Barnsley
South Yorkshire S70 2AS

ISBN 978 1 78337 611 7

Printed and bound in England
by CPI Group (UK) Ltd, Croydon, CR0 4YY

Typeset in Times New Roman by
CHIC GRAPHICS

Pen & Sword Books Ltd incorporates the imprints of Pen & Sword
Archaeology, Atlas, Aviation, Battleground, Discovery,
Family History, History, Maritime, Military, Naval, Politics, Railways,
Select, Social History, Transport, True Crime, Claymore Press,
Frontline Books, Leo Cooper, Praetorian Press, Remember When,
Seaforth Publishing and Wharncliffe.

For a complete list of Pen and Sword titles please contact
Pen and Sword Books Limited
47 Church Street, Barnsley, South Yorkshire, S70 2AS, England
E-mail: enquiries@pen-and-sword.co.uk
Website: www.pen-and-sword.co.uk

Contents

List of Plates

Peasants harvesting wheat, from the *Queen Mary Psalter*. (British Library Illuminated Manuscripts Collection)

Peasants driving oxen and bulls, from the *Queen Mary Psalter*. (British Library Illuminated Manuscripts Collection)

St Francis making his plain brown habit. From *The Taymouth Hours*, early fourteenth century. (British Library Illuminated Manuscripts Collection)

Preacher John Ball and the rebels led by Wat Tyler. (British Library)

Illustration from *Hye-Waye to the Spyttel-House*, c. 1535. (British Library)

The Beggars' Dole, from Rotha Mary Clay, *The Medieval Hospitals of England* (1909). (Wellcome Images Collection)

The Counterfeit Crank, Nicolas Genings. (British Library)

Bridewell Prison in 1720. (Wellcome Images Collection)

Elizabeth Clarke and another witch identify their familiars under interrogation by Witchfinder-General Matthew Hopkins. (Wellcome Images Collection)

A panorama of Bartholomew Fair in 1721. (Wellcome Images Collection)

Colour print of Bartholomew Fair by Thomas Rowlandson, c.1813. (Wellcome Images Collection)

New Bedlam at Moorfields. (Wellcome Images Collection)

Scene from Bedlam in William Hogarth's *Rake's Progress* from 1731. (Wellcome Images Collection).

William Hogarth's 'Gin Lane' of 1751. (Author's collection).

Tyburn, as depicted by William Hogarth.

A view of the Foundling Hospital. (Wellcome Images Collection).

Young country girl Moll is seduced by a brothel keeper, from Hogarth's *Harlot's Progress*. (Wellcome Images Collection)

Bridewell Prison depicted in 1732 in William Hogarth's *Harlot's Progress*. (Wellcome Images Collection)

'A Woman of All Trades', 1792. (Library of Congress)

Billy Waters, the well-known black busker and beggar of London. (Wellcome Images Collection).

Master Toby. (Wellcome Images Collection).

Street entertainer Joseph Johnson. (Wellcome Images Collection).

A spinning wheel and a stocking frame. (Wellcome Images Collection)

Dinner at the Workhouse, 1901. (Author's collection)

Teenage girl selling flowers. (Author's collection)

Crossing-sweeper boys. (Author's collection)

Casuals wait for admission to the workhouse. (Author's collection)

A vagrant in 1846. (Wellcome Images Collection)

Widow and child, 1877. (London School of Economics)

The homeless sleeping out in St James' Park in 1887. (Author's collection)

A section of Charles Booth's poverty map of 1889–98, showing east London. (London School of Economics)

Coffin-style beds in Medland Hall Refuge in east London. (Author's collection)

A common lodging house in Spitalfields. (Author's collection)

Introduction

The word 'pauper' (from the Latin, meaning poor) is rarely used today. For most people it conjures up scenes from the Victorian workhouse and Charles Dickens' *Oliver Twist*; a toothless, raggedy old man stumbling on the treadmill or a hungry, barefooted orphan boy begging for more gruel. It appears to have entered the English language in the early sixteenth century via a legal phrase relating to those unable to pay for their legal fees in court. Using this definition, a pauper is anybody who depends on charity or aid.

In this book the pauper takes centre stage in English History. Kings and Queens are shunted off to the wings along with Prime Ministers and Archbishops. Tales of swashbuckling adventure, military triumph and political chicanery are replaced with the grim details of life in the gutter. There will be filth and foul odours, death and disease, begging and scavenging, Gin-drinking and rioting. There will be monks, crooks and con-artists, buskers, sex workers, immigrants and slaves.

Our story begins in Medieval England when the vast majority of the population were peasants working the land in conditions of near-slavery (Chapter 1). Throughout this period the rich believed or were encouraged to believe by the church that giving alms to the poor would atone for their sins. Some Christian orders even chose to live in poverty in order to follow the teachings of Jesus Christ (Chapter 3). This attitude had definitely changed by the fourteenth century: begging and vagrancy were first criminalised in 1349 in an attempt to crack down on labourers moving around in search of better wages in the aftermath of the Black Death. This conflict eventually resulted in the 'Peasants' Revolt' of 1381 (Chapter 4). The peasants lost, but vagrants continued to increase in number despite increasingly harsh punishments (Chapter 6). This plague of rogues and vagabonds, who chose idleness as a career and faked illness and disability to beg for alms, was thought to threaten national security. In one notorious incident Queen Elizabeth I was riding in the countryside just outside London when 'she was invironed with a Number of begging Rogues, which gave the Queen much Disturbance'. Complaints were made, warrants were issued and seventy-four rogues were arrested: 'some were blind, and yet great Usurers, and very rich'. Their punishment was to be sent to Bridewell Prison (Chapter 8).

The Elizabethan Age also saw the introduction of the 'Poor Law' (Chapter 8), combining punishment of the idle (those who would not work) with relief for the aged and infirm (those who could not work). But how do you distinguish the deserving poor from the undeserving poor? This problem, and the increasing cost of poor relief (Chapter 18), led eventually to the workhouse system and poor law reform of 1834 (Chapter 19). At the same time the state was taking more of the burden for providing for those who depended on charity, including the mentally ill (Chapter 12) and unwanted infants (Chapter 15), while funding the removal of unwanted immigrants (Chapter 20).

On the edges of the pauper class were those who scraped a living in the city by busking, selling flowers and trinkets, sweeping road-crossings, and prostitution (Chapters 16, 17 and 21). Most were looked upon as vagrants of one form or another and faced being hauled into court and shipped off to prison.

Some light relief is provided by the popular amusements to be found at St Bartholomew's Fair staged outside the hospital for the poor (Chapter 11). And of course there was always the option of finding pleasure (or drowning sorrows) in drink (Chapter 14).

Where possible, the paupers of this book speak in their own words or at least the words attributed to them in contemporary sources (details are given at the end of the book). This is obviously more difficult in the earlier chapters, which have to rely on sources such as the Domesday Book, historical accounts by the literate and wealthy classes, court reports, poems and other works of literature which may or may not be based on fact. In the seventeenth and eighteenth centuries we start to see the first examples of what we might now call investigative journalism with accounts of visits to asylums and workhouses (even if they are written to entertain rather than inform).

INTRODUCTION

By the nineteenth century newspapers were full of factual reports and undercover exposes and in the 1880s it became fashionable for the upper classes to go 'slumming' for themselves in the East End of London.

In some ways this book resembles a slumming tour through the last 1,000 years of English History. It attempts to insert the reader into the action rather than simply describe events. In some episodes this involves taking the role of a visitor to an insane asylum or a journalist investigating a workhouse casual ward. In others it means imagining we are travelling through Norman England, donning the robes of a Franciscan monk or taking part in the Peasants' Revolt. The idea behind this approach is to get a better insight to a pauper's life between 1066 and the beginning of the Welfare State in the early twentieth century. Some of the issues raised remain just as relevant today.

CHAPTER 1

Domesday

In which we journey through Norman England from Winchester to Gloucester twenty years after the Battle of Hastings

The ceremony begins. In the middle of the marketplace a slave stands before his lord, the man who owns his body and controls where he lives, works and sleeps. In one hand the slave holds the symbol of his bondage; a sickle used to harvest the crops, a goad for prodding the cattle, or some other farming tool. In the other hand he holds 30 pence in coin. This is the price of his freedom, the literal 'value of his skin'. Once the money is handed over to his lord in the presence of suitable witnesses, the slave puts down his tool and takes up a sword, a lance or another symbol of his new status. He is no longer a slave. He is now a freeman.

Slavery has been part of English life for centuries. It existed before the Roman invasion. It continued under the Anglo-Saxon kings. And while the custom is gradually dying out, there are still many slaves living under our new Norman rulers. The survey being carried out throughout this year (AD 1086) will show that there are more than 25,000 slaves among the 268,863 people counted. Although the survey does not include family members and the inhabitants of the major cities of London and Winchester, it suggests that slaves account for as much as 10 per cent of the total population of England (guessed to be around two million). Most appear to work as ploughmen or household servants. They may have been born into slavery, or taken captive during a raid or war. They may have been enslaved as a punishment for a crime. They may have been sold into slavery by their poor families or even volunteered themselves as a last resort.

Slavery may be dying out slowly but many of the peasant classes above them are hardly 'free'. Most are required to pay rent and work a set amount for their landlord before they can produce anything for themselves. Just like the slave, they are punished if they attempt to run away or move without consent of their lord. Under Anglo-Saxon law if a captured fugitive cannot pay his lord 60 shillings then he becomes a slave. The penalty for killing your lord is to be tortured, scalped or disembowelled (or a combination of all three).

The largest group among the peasantry are the 'un-free' villeins (40 per cent of the population) who on average have 30 acres of land and two plough oxen. Next come the poorer bordars (30 per cent) and cottars or cottagers who generally own between one and five acres of land, just enough to feed their family. For them an ox would be a luxury.

Freemen (14 per cent of the population) are mainly found in the Viking-influenced north and own an average of 30 acres and two oxen. They are mostly rent-paying tenant farmers who do not have to perform extra duties for the lord of the manor. Some may be better off than the villein but others suffer a 'wretched and miserable' life. It is thought their numbers are decreasing as the Normans impose their rule upon the country.

The most significant change brought about by the invasion was the replacement of Anglo-Saxon nobles with Norman ones. It is argued that the rest of society remains much the same and is divided into three sections; those who pray, those who fight, and those who work. At the top is King William, followed by his lords and the chiefs who hold the land in his name. At the bottom are the peasants who work on the land and make up 95 per cent of the population. If a person has no land to work and no lord then he is found one.

* * *

We can see some of the effects of the Norman invasion as we make our 80-mile journey between the major cities of Winchester and Gloucester. Winchester is the old Anglo-Saxon capital of England

and the burial place of King Alfred the Great. While London is larger (estimated population 10,000), Winchester remains the administrative capital and the location of the treasury. Taking the Broadway into the heart of Winchester we can see the new cathedral being built using limestone from the Isle of Wight. Near the west gate stands William the Conqueror's castle, built on land freed up by the destruction of fifty Anglo-Saxon homes. It is a reminder of the devastation wrought upon England by the Norman invaders over the last twenty years, burning down Canterbury and York, razing the ports, building castles and monasteries, and imposing taxes and tolls. There are reports of harsh weather, dying crops, pestilence, famine and death, particularly in the north. Supporters of the new regime will however tell you that the roads are now so safe that a girl laden with gold could travel from one end of the country to the other without fear.

The Normans themselves are notorious for their love of arms and horses, hunting and hawking. Unlike the hairy Anglo-Saxons, the Normans shave their faces and the back of their necks. They are also distinguished by their wealth, their silks and furs and their French tongue. It will be another 350 years before English is recognised as the language of government again.

From Winchester we set off towards Andover along the straight road set out by the Romans hundreds of years ago through gently undulating countryside dotted with small farms, towns and villages. To our right is Headborne Worthy. The ploughland and meadows here were once held by King Harold, Earl of Wessex, and the Saxon lord Cypping. Now the peasants here serve the Normans Ralph de Mortimer and Bernard Pauncevolt. To the left is Littleton, granted to Hugh de Port after the Conquest. To the victor goes the spoils.

Then comes Chibolton. The land here has always belonged to the monastery, and now belongs to Walkelin, the first Norman bishop of Winchester.

On arriving at Andover we learn that the surveyors have recorded 107 male inhabitants, six watermills grinding grain into flour, 18 acres of meadow and enough woodland for 100 pigs. In the King's land there are sixty-two villeins, thirty-six bordars, three freemen and six slaves with twenty-four ploughs.

Seeing one of the slaves at work with the plough, we decide to ask him a few questions. Alf is of Saxon appearance, with a fringe and short hair cut at the back rather than shaved. He is perhaps 5ft 7in tall, with small feet clad in simple shoes cut from leather. He is wearing a knee-length tunic beneath a short cloak, secured at the front. His legs are bare, although he might wrap a few rags around them in winter. He has a wife and two sons, one of whom works the land with him. He has a twelve-year-old daughter, who within a couple of years will be married, most likely to another ploughman on the manor. Their home is made of timber, perhaps 20ft by 10ft, with a hearth in the middle.

'So, ploughman, is this hard work?' we ask.

'Oh I work very hard indeed, sir. It's more than my life is worth to stay at home – not with the landlord I've got. As soon as the sun rises I drive the oxen out to the field and yoke them to the plough. I have to plough a full acre or more every day.'

'Do you work with anyone else?'

'My eldest son drives the oxen with his goad, although he can hardly speak today what with the cold and all the shouting at the animals to keep them at it.'

'Do you have any other duties?'

'Sure I have. A lot more. I have to water the oxen, fill up their stable with hay and take their dung out. It's hard work all right, sir, but I don't have a choice, because I am not free.'

Disheartened by his gloomy tone, we leave the fields, stopping only to view the dead crows hung above the fields to scare off other birds. At the stable we find the oxherd, who takes the oxen out to pasture when the ploughman has finished.

'I work hard for my lord too,' he says. 'I stand over the oxen from dusk until dawn to prevent the thieves getting at them and then I make sure the beasts are well fed and watered ready for the day's work.'

We bid good day to the workers in the fields and plough our own route past the Savernake Forest to Marlborough. We can see the motte and bailey castle – a castle on top of a mound of earth surrounded by a wall – still being fortified. Next on our route is Cirencester, once the second largest city in Roman Britain. Here the land is owned by Regenbald, one of the few Englishman who profited from the conquest because he was once chaplain to Edward the Confessor, King William's cousin. He also owns land in Berkshire, Herefordshire, Dorset, Somerset and Buckinghamshire.

From Cirencester we take the Roman Road north-west to Gloucester, our final destination. Once the capital of Mercia, and home to the palace of Edward the Confessor, it now holds perhaps as many as 3,000 people. Its Roman walls still stand and, like Marlborough, it too has a Norman motte and bailey castle, built on land once occupied by sixteen Saxon houses.

Gloucester was also the birthplace of the survey that is taking place across the while country. In the winter of 1085 King William gathered his most trusted men here together for a council. After much discussion it was decided to send out his men across every shire of England to find out who owned the land and what the land was worth.

We can see part of the process in the county court. Men from every part of the shire have gathered here to give their evidence to the King's Commissioners. There are barons, landlords, priests, the reeve (who oversees the peasants) and villeins from each 'hundred', which is a Saxon term referring to the amount of land which can support 100 households. Gloucestershire is made up of forty such hundreds.

As we enter the King's Commissioners, Remigius the Bishop of Lincoln, Henry de Ferrars, Walter Giffard, and Adam, brother of Eudes the Steward, are questioning the men of Langley hundred, perhaps 30 miles to the south-west of Gloucester, about the manor of Alveston. They are interested in the taxable value of the land (divided into units called hides) and the division of ploughs between those attached to the manor and those used by the peasants.

'Who held it in the time of King Edward?'
'Earl Harold.'
'How many hides?'
'Ten.'

'Ploughs?'
'Three in demesne, twenty-two with the men.'
'How many men?'
'Twenty-three villeins, five bordars and two slaves.'
'Has anything been added since?'
'The reeve has added two ploughs and five slaves.'
'How much is it worth?'
'Twelve pounds.'

Next comes Thornbury, the market town just north of Alveston. This was once held by Beorhtric, son of Aelfgar, when there was eleven hides, four ploughs on the lord's land, forty-two villeins and eighteen radknights with twenty-one ploughs, and twenty-four bordars and fifteen slaves and four freemen. 'Radknights' – meaning riding men – are free men belonging to the upper ranks of the peasantry who act as an escort for their lord, who is now Humphrey, the King's Chamberlain.

The call then goes up for the manor of Woodchester – but it seems nobody has turned up to give evidence to the Commissioners. There are only the men from Longtree hundred, who explain that the land was once held by Gytha, the mother of Earl Harold, and is now held by Edward of Salisbury for King William.

Examining the records for Gloucester we see other inhabitants listed besides peasants, ploughs and pigs. At the top of the list of landowners is 'Rex Willelmus' – King William. Under the king comes the Archbishop of York, the bishops of Hereford and Worcester, the abbots and the Norman lords. There is Berdic, the King's jester, who owns three villages and five ploughs in the Welsh marches, and pays no tax. And also a William the Scribe, who has one messuage (house and garden) worth 51 pence. William is a common name at this time, and there are other entries such as William the Bald, William the Priest and even William the Goat.

Eventually the information concerning Gloucestershire will be written down neatly in Latin, with red ink for the headings and place markers and black ink for the rest. Once combined with the information from the other regions it will not only give King William an idea of the value of his kingdom, but also provide people in the future with an insight into life in England in the eleventh century.

By the twelfth century the book containing this information became known by the English natives as 'Domesday', as in the day of judgement. The Domesday Book was never finished. In fact there are two books. The larger one of 800 pages covers the whole of England except for Essex, Norfolk and Suffolk. There are also gaps left for the missing descriptions of London, Winchester and Hastings. A second volume, smaller in size but with 900 pages, contains a more detailed account of the missing section of Essex, Norfolk and Suffolk. Historians are divided on the question of why the Domesday Book was not finished – one theory is that it was cut short by King William's death on 9 September 1087.

CHAPTER 2

The King of the Poor

*In which the bearded revolutionary William FitzOsbert attempts
to stir up a revolt of the poor and middle classes against the
wealthy citizens of London in 1196*

The King of the Poor stands before a large assembly of Londoners in
the shadow of St Paul's Cathedral. He wears no crown but is
immediately recognisable by his long bushy beard, even in the midst
of a city as densely populated as the new capital of England. How
many of those 25,000 souls have turned out to hear Longbeard speak?
We find it impossible to count, hemmed in on all sides by shopkeepers,
tradesmen, labourers and common paupers. All appear rapt by his
words, occasionally cheering and shouting out in approval. Let us
listen:

'. . . with joy shall ye draw water out of the wells of salvation . . . I
am the saviour of the poor. Do ye, oh, poor, who have experienced the
heaviness of rich men's hands, drink from my wells the waters of
salvation, and ye may do this joyfully . . .'

Longbeard raises his hands, his face quivering with righteous fury.

'For the time of your visitation is at hand, for I will divide the
waters from the waters. The people are the waters. I will divide the
humble from the haughty and treacherous. I will separate the elect
from the reprobate, as light from darkness.'

The quotations from Scripture tumble out one after another, making
it hard to decipher the meaning and purpose of his speech. Gradually
it becomes clearer. Longbeard's anger is directed at the leaders of this
city, the 'optimates', the wealthy oligarchy of lords, bishops and
merchant families, the mayor and his sheriffs who rule this city as if

it were an independent state. In return they pay a yearly rent of £300 to King Richard. Longbeard claims their arrogance – and their treason – is compounded by their failure to pay a fair share of the King's taxes. These miserly businessmen spare their own fortunes while the common man is forced to dig deep to pay for Richard's war in France. Why should the poor shopkeeper in his wooden house pay the same as the rich merchant in his stone fortress? Should not every man pay a proportion of what he can afford? Look around you at this splendid city, says Longbeard. All around us is proof that there is one rule for the rich, cloaked in their silks and furs, fattened on goose, guinea-hen and woodcock, and another for the poor, bent double with their unequal burden, caked in the excrement of their so-called betters.

This contrast between rich and poor is mirrored by two different descriptions of London, the city which has now replaced Winchester as the economic and political capital of England. Firstly, this is the city described by William Fitzstephen as the seat of the English monarchy, one 'whose renown is more widespread, whose money and merchandise go further afield, and which stands head and shoulders above the others', famous too for 'the wholesomeness of its climate, the devotion of its Christians, the strength of its fortifications, its well-situated location, the respectability of its citizens, and the propriety of their wives'. This is the city built upon 'that greatest of rivers, the Thames', whose banks are lined with ships, storerooms and shops offering the finest French wines, gold from Arabia, spice from Sabaea, palm oil from Babylon, steel from Scythia, gems from the Nile, crimson silks from China, and fish, fowl and game from all corners of the land. This is the city blessed with Westminster Abbey (completed just six years ago) and St Paul's Cathedral (as yet unfinished), and more than 100 churches catering for the spiritual needs of its citizens. Its virtues stretch beyond its walls too, in the suburbs rich in beautiful gardens, rich farmland, clear springs and vast forests abundant in wild stags, boars and bulls. No wonder that almost all the bishops, abbots and lords of England live here, for every need is satisfied: hunting with falcons, hawks and hounds; cockfighting and boar, bear and bull-baiting; archery, wrestling, athletics, shotput and javelin; war games and jousting, both on field and on river; and football, the sport that almost every adolescent engages in after work or school.

Then there is the darker version of Richard of Devizes: 'There is not a single street in it that does not abound in miserable, obscene wretches,' he warns. 'Behold! I warn you, whatever of evil or of perversity there is in any, whatever in all parts of the world, you will find in that city alone.' Here are common beggars and vagrants; drinkers and druggists; actors, flatterers, panders and pickpockets; gamblers, fortune-tellers, extortioners, magicians and mimics; the lewd and lustful dancing girls, streetwalkers, catamites, sodomites, girl-boys and men who have plucked every hair from their body. It is said that there are more braggadocios in London than in all France.

King Richard is said to have declared that he would sell London if he could find a buyer. Instead it was sold to the citizens themselves. In 1191, while the Lionheart was abroad on his Crusade, the leading nobles negotiated with his brother John to secure the freedom of the city and reduce their annual payment to the Crown. Two years later, when the King was held hostage by the King of France until an extortionate ransom was paid, the wealthiest citizens attempted to avoid paying their fair share towards the total.

Longbeard, ever loyal to King Richard, claims to have witnessed this treachery first hand. He tells the crowd of a meeting he witnessed at his own brother's stone house in 1194. One noble, Robert Brand, declared that 'London shall have no king except their mayor', while another expressed the hope that the Lionheart never return home. Even Longbeard's brother Richard FitzOsbert rejected the need to pay royal taxes to fund the war in Normandy. So Longbeard approached the King and accused Richard FitzOsbert of high treason. The King, who knew of Longbeard's distinguished service during the Third Crusade, listened to his complaint but took no action against the supposed traitors. Years later, when Longbeard discovered the lengths that the nobles were taking to avoid tax, he travelled to France once more to inform King Richard. Perhaps encouraged by the King's reply, he began criticising the city leaders – the so-called 'optimates' – at every public meeting. He encouraged the poorer citizens to rebel against

21

iniquity and injustice and demand a fairer system of taxation.

The oligarchs, who had previously thought Longbeard was one of their own, spread their own propaganda. William FitzOsbert was no champion of the poor, they said, but a man of privilege, a lawyer, the son of a wealthy clerk. His complaints were nothing to do with concern for the common man but about his own dwindling resources. Having frittered away the best part of his inheritance on his lavish lifestyle and a devoted concubine, Longbeard now wanted to steal from his brother and his brother's friends. Pride and envy drove him to take to the streets and call public meeting after public meeting, inflaming everyone from the needy up to the only-moderately-wealthy with a desire for 'unbounded liberty and happiness'. Longbeard's rabble-rousing, they claimed, was just part of a conspiracy to take over the city. Rumours spread that Longbeard is planning to break into the stone houses of the rich and seize the silver that they have attempted to conceal from the taxman.

Faced with mounting unrest, the Lord Archbishop of Canterbury Hubert Walter, who was appointed to rule over England as 'Justiciar' in the King's absence, travelled to London with his troops to restore order. He summoned Longbeard to answer to a charge of treason but was forced to retreat when confronted by the King of the Poor's supporters.

Walter decided a more devious plan was required. So he personally addressed a congregation of Londoners and asked them to prove their loyalty to King Richard by offering hostages from every ward of the city to keep the peace. They had little choice but to agree. Walter also announced that any Londoners found outside the city would be arrested as enemies of the state.

The Justiciar's next move takes place before our own eyes.

Longbeard draws his speech to a close with the promise that he will call another meeting tomorrow, and the day after that, until the optimates agree to their demands for a fairer system. The people disperse, returning to their homes or their families, or the inn or gaming house. Longbeard now stands nearly alone with the woman he loves and a few scattered companions. It is at this moment that the

Justiciar's men strike. Two nobles armed with an axe and a sword quickly confront William FitzOsbert and attempt to take him by force. Longbeard has no intention of backing down. He wrests the axe from one magnate, reverses the blade and slays the man with a single blow. The remaining noble is quickly dispatched by one of Longbeard's associates.

The King of the Poor escapes as the alarm is raised. What next? Surely the Justiciar will send in the troops? Is the promised revolution at hand?

* * *

The next day, Sunday 6 April 1196, we travel to the place that Longbeard has chosen for his final stand: the church of St Mary-le-Bow on Cheapside, the financial centre of London. The neighbouring streets are also evidence of its importance as a marketplace: Bread Street, Milk Street, Wood Street, Honey Lane, Ironmonger Lane and Poultry. The church itself – also known as St Mary de Arcubus because of its two prominent arches – is perhaps the best location Longbeard could have chosen outside of the Tower of London. For while it is not an easily-defended fortress, it is a landmark that he hopes will attract the multitudes of the city to his cause. He can also use the bells which would otherwise ring out the eight o'clock curfew.

Longbeard hopes that the people will respond to his calls now as they did before to rescue him from the Archbishop's forces. But we can see only the massed ranks of Walter's troops surrounding the church. Longbeard's supporters – estimated by some at 52,000 – have stayed at home rather than risk the lives of those handed over as hostages.

The troops order Longbeard to come out of his sanctuary and surrender. The King of the Poor refuses. After a short siege, the troops move forward with burning torches and set the doors and shuttered windows ablaze. Then, when the main door is weakened by fire, the troops hack their way inside. Shouts are heard and a few minutes later, Longbeard and his eight co-conspirators are dragged out into the street.

Longbeard's stomach has been cut open with a knife in the struggle and blood stains his tunic. He knows his death is at hand and it will not be pretty.

We watch as the armed procession takes him down Cheapside, King William Street and East Cheap towards the Tower, a 'royal fortress of tremendous size and strength'.

* * *

The trial, if you could call it that, is swift. Longbeard confesses under torture to his treachery and even to sacrilege by his 'carnal intercourse' with his lover in the church. Worse still, he admits that in the moments before his capture he cursed Jesus Christ and appealed to Satan as his Saviour. He and his companions are condemned to be hanged in the most bloodthirsty fashion reserved for traitors. They are stripped and their hands tied behind their back. Long ropes are tied from their feet to a team of horses which draw them through the middle of the city to the elms at Smithfield, leaving a trail of bloody flesh along more than a mile of highway. Before a crowd of Londoners Longbeard's body is ripped apart and hanged in chains on a gibbet, a visceral warning to those who dare to oppose the rulers of this city and the kingdom.

Although few have heard of Longbeard's exploits, at the time he was regarded by some as a martyr and patron saint of London, just like Thomas à Becket, the former Archbishop of Canterbury. Like Longbeard, Becket was arrested as he sheltered in a church. Becket was also a favourite of the common people of London and made a point of donating his luxuries to the poor while he observed a diet of plain bread and fennel water. After he was murdered on the orders of King Richard's father Henry II in 1170, his blood was said to cure sickness and so many miracles were reported that he was canonised only three years after his death. Similar marvels were told about Longbeard after his execution. It was reported that so many pilgrims flocked to the scene to wash their hands in his blood and scrape away the earth beneath the hanging corpse that it quickly became a large ditch. The chains that bound his body were removed from the scene by a priest and are said to have instantly relieved a fever. The gibbet was also taken away, possibly to be worshipped in secret. It became such an embarrassment that the city leaders ordered that anybody who went there to pray would be arrested and whipped.

Although he is now nowhere near as famous as Becket, he may not have died in vain. It is likely the city leaders recognised part of his complaint about taxation (which may have been collected at a flat rate regardless of wealth or income). By 1199 the rate was recorded at four shillings per pound of rateable value for owners of stone-built properties and two shillings for thatched properties. Anyone with less than two shillings in rent or chattels did not have to pay anything. Foreigners were no longer exempt.

CHAPTER 3

Mendicants

*In which we experience the wilful poverty of Franciscan
friars after their arrival in England in the early
thirteenth century*

Take off your fancy shoes. Remove your linen, your furs and silk. And
your ribbons and veils. Say farewell to your gold and jewels. Your new
clothing will be a simple woollen robe. A cord and breeches if you
wish. It is time to forsake all your possessions and renounce your
pursuit of earthly wealth and power. As Jesus said: 'If you wish to be
perfect, go, sell everything you have and give it to the poor and you
will have treasure in heaven.'

With these words the friar welcomes us into the brotherhood of St
Francis of Assisi. He calls himself William of Nottingham, and he is
not at all like the jolly fat monk of legend. If we did not know him to
be a priest, we might have thought he was a common beggar in the
street, so emaciated is his frame and deathly is his pallor. Not that
Brother William would object to this comparison: his life is devoted
to Lady Poverty, and lepers and beggars are his natural companions.
Perhaps the only things that set him apart are his tonsure – the practice
of shaving the hair from the top of the scalp, leaving an odd-looking
circular fringe.

He ushers us into a small chamber at the back of the schoolhouse
at the hospital of Poor Priests in the city of Canterbury. It was in the
cathedral here, rebuilt by William the Conqueror and lavishly adorned
with glass windows, marble floors, coloured paintings and a panelled
ceiling, that Thomas à Becket was murdered. By contrast, the

Franciscans' new home is anything but luxurious. The chamber has been divided into tiny cells in which each man can sleep after a long day mingling with the very poorest of the land. There are no comfortable beds or pillows – for according to the Gospel of Matthew, Jesus had nowhere to lay his head.

From there we are led into the schoolhouse, where the friars have gathered around a fire. A small pot is handed to us, at the bottom of which is a thick, warm liquid that smells like mud but tastes a lot like beer. Sour beer. 'I have seen the brethren drink beer of such sourness that some preferred to drink water,' says Brother William. Occasionally they eat the round flatbread known as torta, and on three days of the week are permitted to accept meat and fish from the kind people of the city.

When we ask why they have chosen to live like this, Brother William looks surprised. Have we not heard the story of Francis of Assisi in Italy? Francis was the son of a rich merchant who as a young boy dreamed of fame and fortune as a valiant knight. It was during one such expedition that he heard the voice of God ask him: 'Why do you leave the Master for the servant?' Francis knew he had to return to Assisi and devote himself to serving our Lord. And so it was, little by little, that he dedicated himself to the needs of the poor. On a pilgrimage to Rome he borrowed the clothes of a beggar and spent the day outside St Peter's church asking for alms. He gave away food. He embraced a leper and gave him money. He believed that the human desire for material possessions led only to violence, oppression and misery. It was for that reason that Francis renounced his worldly possessions. All those who follow him must do the same.

Are only men allowed to join the order? No. Women may join the Lesser Sisters of St Clare, one of the first followers. Clare was a nobleman's daughter who ran away from home to join St Francis, at an age when other ladies would be contemplating marriage.

Curious, we ask about the rules by which they live. The most important, we learn, is that Franciscans must live in the spirit of poverty. That means they must always be pilgrims and strangers wherever they are, with no title nor possessions.

'We must also fast and abstain from vices and sins and from superfluity of food and drink, and be catholics,' says William. 'We must also deny ourselves and put our bodies under the yoke of servitude and holy obedience as each one has promised to the Lord.'

The brothers dress only in humble, undyed cloth, with perhaps a lamb's wool jacket in colder weather. They cannot carry lethal weapons. Coins should be handled only when they are given away, or as Brother William puts it: 'A brother would not sin who handled money in distributing the alms of others to the poor.' Meat is allowed only on Sundays, Tuesdays and Thursdays, and dinner should always be preceded by the Lord's Prayer. Speaking of which, there are seven Hours of prayer – Matins (morning), Prime (the first hour after dawn), Terce (the third hour), Sext (the sixth hour), None (the ninth hour), Vespers (sunset) and Compline. Sins should be confessed three times a year and attendance at unseemly parties, shows or dances is forbidden. William also explains that a friar cannot leave unless he is expelled for bad behaviour or enters another religious order.

As to their ramshackle accommodation, William tells us that it is only temporary, as they have only recently arrived in England. Francis appointed Brother Agnellus of Pisa to lead four clerics and five lay brethren, including several Englishmen, to cross the Channel. They landed on September 10, 1224, in the eighth year of King Henry, son of King John. Four days later, perhaps in recognition of his work, Francis received the stigmata, the five wounds of Christ.

Four of this happy band travelled to London, where they rented a house in Cornhill, while the others remained in Canterbury. From there the brothers spread far and wide, to York and to Oxford, where the brothers built their own church by hand using stones and sand.

Brother William tells us of the novice Solomon, who followed the rule of poverty so strictly that he starved himself to death. His foot became infected, his spine became hunched and bent, and he suffered dropsy and bleeding haemorrhoids until he finally rose up to sweet Jesus in heaven. 'On the day before his soul went forth unto his lord, he was cast into such sorrow of heart that all the sufferings he had hitherto borne seemed nothing in comparison with his agony,' said William.

He smiles as we shiver at the thought of so much suffering and reminds us of the example of Jesus Christ, who died for our salvation. 'Men lose all that they leave behind in this world,' he says, 'but they carry with them the reward of charity and the alms which they gave, for which they will receive from the Lord a recompense and worthy remuneration.'

Francis of Assisi died in October 1226 and was pronounced a saint two years later by Pope Gregory IX. His teachings are said to have brought rich and poor closer together and given the poor and oppressed a sense of dignity. The Franciscans eventually moved into a new church on an island on the river Stour. There they remained until 1358 and the dissolution of the monasteries and friaries under Henry VIII.

CHAPTER 4

Black Death

*In which we stumble into an abandoned village afflicted
by the Great Mortality of 1348 and learn of its effects
on the common people*

Death greets us with an eerie silence. This village would normally be alive with noise – ploughmen shouting at their oxen in the fields, shopkeepers advertising their wares, carts trundling to town and back, people greeting each other in the street and children playing in the mud. We see and hear none of this as we approach. Instead an acrid stench stings the back of our nostrils. Smoke rises from piles of ashes of who-knows-what. The small church is empty. A message scrawled on the wall reads: 'Wretched, terrible, destructive year. The remnants of the people alone remain.'

We see these remnants now, piled in a heap in a trench at the back of the graveyard, the bodies of men, women and children, black and swollen with decay. The smell alone is evidence of a fearsome disease and prevents us from examining them closer. If there is anyone left in this village it seems they have neither the will nor energy to give their fellow residents a proper burial. Or till the fields, it seems. The land beyond the church appears ripe for harvesting, the grain weighs down heavily upon the stalks. Elsewhere sheep, goats and cows wander about with not an owner in sight.

Then out of the corner of our eye we detect movement. An unusually tall figure shambles into view, heading towards the church. After a few moments we see that it is a man with a child perched upon his shoulders. But this is no happy family scene. The man, barely clothed in tattered rags, stumbles from left to right, as if drunk, while the child's sags lifelessly. We call out a greeting but there is no reply, only a vacant, zombie stare. Now that he is closer we see the large swelling the size of an apple under his left armpit oozing a bloody black pus. As he reaches the common burial pit he lifts the child from his shoulders and drops it on top of the other bodies. A murmur escapes his lips as he stares at his son lying dead, victim of the same plague that now ravages him, before he turns and shambles back to the road. His feet carry him a few paces before he collapses to the ground. We cannot help him now. It is too late for that.

Resisting the urge to flee from this place in terror we head towards any peasant home that looks like it might still be inhabited. Surely there are some survivors, sheltering behind locked doors? One such wooden house, tidily presented with a thatched roof and window shutters bears no sign that it has been touched by pestilence. We undo the latch on the front door and peer inside until our eyes are accustomed to the gloom. There is nobody here in this single room of around 13ft square – only a small wooden table with a few scraps of barley bread and a dormant fireplace. The dirt floor is covered with straw and in the corner there is a mattress made of fern and heather. Outside, the latrine – little more than a hole in the ground – is overflowing with water, faeces and rubbish. The owners of this place have either died or run away in search of cleaner air or aid and medicine in nearby towns or cities.

Other houses have been burnt to the ground in an attempt to cleanse them of the disease. It seems we are the only living human beings in this village.

All the omens suggest that is time to leave.

* * *

What is this plague? People experience it in different forms, but for most it begins with a headache, rising temperature, vomiting, dizziness, sensitivity to light and sleeplessness. After a day or two the painful swellings appear in the armpit or groin – a sure sign that death

31

is near. In desperation, some attempt to cut them open or burn them with hot irons. Others try leeches or poultices of mustard, figs and onions. The doctors have plenty of answers but no cures – they recommend burning fires of laurel or camomile, drinking broth seasoned with ground pepper, ginger and cloves, frequent purging of the stomach through vomiting and strict chastity (for human sin is the obvious explanation for the plague). Bloodletting may also assist – try opening the vein in the thumb if the bubo is located on the neck or the vein in the middle finger if it is under the armpit. One doctor believes the poison can be sucked out by pressing the plucked anus of a live chicken against the swelling until the bird chokes and dies.

Writers call it the Great Mortality (no one has yet invented the term 'Black Death') and it is unlike anything that has gone before. Not even the Great Famine of 30-odd years ago can compare. Back then, in 1315, the failure of successive harvests left the poor so hungry that they ate dogs, cats, birds and – some say – even their own children. The dead went unburied and the living were so desperate that they begged, stole and murdered to ensure their survival. 'Alas land of England! You who out of your abundance once helped other lands, now, poor and needy, are forced to beg,' wrote one chronicler about the famine. 'A fruitful land is turned into barrenness.'

Is the disease caused a corruption of the atmosphere, a sign of God's displeasure or the result of a foul conjunction of Saturn, Jupiter and Mars? Do we believe the verdict of one archbishop that it is caused by 'the sins of men who, made callous by prosperity, neglect to remember the benefits of the Supreme Giver'? This sickness has claimed priests and doctors as well as sinners, rich as well as poor. Even the new Archbishop of Canterbury, Thomas Bradwardine himself, has fallen prey to the contagion.

All seem convinced that the plague began far to the east in India or Tartary before spreading to the Saracens, the Jews and then the Christians of Europe. As to how it came to England, some believe arrived at the port of Melcombe in Dorset on a ship from Gascony in June of 1348 before spreading along the south coast. Others suggest it hit Southampton first. All agree on its devastation. By the end of the year it had spread along the coast to Devon, Cornwall and Bristol, and inland to Winchester and London. At Gloucester the citizens attempted to shut out the disease by closing the gates. It was futile. By the spring of 1349 it had arrived in Lincoln and York. In Bath, the bishop wrote to his rectors, vicars and priests informing them of the shortage of priests to visit the sick and administer the sacraments. 'If the sick are not able to obtain any priest they should make confession of their sins even to a layman, and if not, a woman.' The Bishop of Winchester suggested the clergy and their congregations should gather for processions around the marketplace or through churchyards while reciting prayers. And still they keep dying, so many that new graveyards have to be opened up away from the centre of town.

At Leicester, for example, the churches no longer have enough priests to take confession, crops rot in the fields for want of harvesting and lords of the manor struggle to find enough servants and the prices of everything have plummeted through lack of demand. Even monasteries, which could usually be relied on to give alms to the poorest, have closed their doors. Meanwhile sheep and cattle wander around aimlessly with nobody to round them up and the value of animals has plummeted. A good horse once worth 40 shillings now only fetches eight, while a cow can be had for 12 pence and a fat sheep for 4 pence.

Yet in some ways the common worker has benefited from the plague. The landless now have plenty of options – and with labour so scarce they can argue for higher wages or better contracts. If the lord of the manor refuses, the tenant can find landowners who are prepared to offer reduced rents, perhaps even at two-thirds or a half of the previous level.

This state of affairs is not welcomed by the ruling classes, who think the workmen 'arrogant and greedy'. The latest order of the King dated 18 June 1349, complains that 'many will not serve unless they may receive excessive wages, and some prefer to beg in idleness than earn their living by labour'.

From now on anyone under 60 who does not have a trade or his own land, whether freeman or slave, is required to serve whoever requires him to, and at the wages he received before the plague struck. If they refuse they face imprisonment. No craftsman can charge a higher price than he did before, whether they be saddlers, skinners, cordwainers, tailors, smiths, masons, tilers or carters. As for butchers, brewers, bakers, fishmongers and other sellers, they must offer their goods for 'a reasonable price' or face having to pay double the amount back to the buyer.

Have they followed the King's orders? It is thought that many have run away and hidden in the woods and forests. Others have been arrested, fined and forced to swear that they will work for the old daily rate and no more.

Even the common beggar is not spared under this new regime. No longer will they be able to 'give themselves to idleness and vice, and sometime to theft and other abominations', says the King. They too will be put to work or face imprisonment. As for the poor lepers, who cannot possibly work and must survive on alms, they are already banned from London to prevent them bothering the nobles, state officials and clergy who travel between Westminster and the City.

In short, the message of the King to his people, spread throughout the land by the officials of the church, is that they should know their place.

The Ordinance of 1349 was followed by the Statute of Labourers in 1351 which again attempted to enforce controls on labour and prices. Discontent continued to grow during the next thirty years before erupting in the Peasants' Revolt of 1381 (see next chapter). As a result, the Black Death is seen as the beginning of a new era, redistributing wealth away from the aristocracy to merchants and even labourers and kick-starting the breakdown of the feudal system. It is estimated to have killed up to half the five million population of England, although some experts put the figure much lower. The plague continued to return sporadically throughout the fifteenth to the sixteenth centuries but it was not until the late nineteenth and early twentieth centuries that scientists established the cause: the bacterium yersinia pestis, *transmitted by a flea feeding on rats.*

CHAPTER 5

Rebellion

*In which we meet the radical preacher John Ball
before witnessing the Peasants' Revolt of 1381
and its brutal suppression*

The guard leads us to a small stone cell, unlatches the heavy wooden door and ushers us inside. We have come to meet the man they call the Mad Priest of Kent, locked up in the dungeon at the Archbishops' palace at Maidstone. This is John Ball – agent of sedition, enemy of the state, a man judged so dangerous he must spend the rest of his life behind bars. A man who promised his gaolers that he would soon be released by an army of peasants 20,000 strong.

So far as we can tell, his madness is now confined to writing letters. A pile of them lie completed on his desk already, with another underway. It is only when the cell door closes behind us that Ball looks up from beneath the robes of the mendicant orders.

Here is one of the messages written by the Mad Priest.

John Ball greets you all and tells you to understand that he has rung your bell. Now let there be right and might, will and skill. God motivate every idler! Now is the time. Lady, send to Jesu your Son, and your Son to his Father, to make a good end. In the name of the Trinity of what is begun! Amen, amen for love, amen!

And a second:

Jack Trueman tells you to understand that falseness and guile have reigned too long; Truth's been set under lock and falseness reigns in every flock

It is likely that letters like these have spread from village to village across the country. For now is the time.

The time for what? John Ball explains, in a sermon he must have given many times before:

My friends, the state of England cannot be right until everything is held communally, and until there is no distinction between nobleman and serf, and we are all as one. Why are those whom we call lords masters over us? How have they deserved it? By what right to they keep us enslaved? We are all descended from our first parents, Adam and Eve; how then can they say that they are better lords than us, except in making us toil and earn for them to spend? They are dressed in velvet and furs, while we wear only cloth. They have wine, and spices and good bread, while we have rye, and straw that has been thrown away, and water to drink. They have fine houses and manors, and we have to brave the wind and rain as we toil in the fields. It is by the sweat of our brows that they maintain their high state. We are called serfs and we are beaten if we do not perform our tasks.

It is this message that has seen him arrested three times and two months ago imprisoned for sedition on the orders of Simon of Sudbury, Archbishop of Canterbury. John Ball's vision of the future is a 'Great Society' in which there will be no lawyers, bishops or lords – only a king and his subjects, free and equal. It does not matter that King Richard is only a boy of 14.

'He is young, and we will show him our miserable slavery, we will tell him it must be changed, or else we will provide the remedy ourselves,' explains John Ball. 'When the king sees us, either he will listen to us, or we will help ourselves.'

England is changing and its peasants have glimpsed the possibility of a life free of feudal obligation, at a wage they can choose to accept or decline. Instead they are branded idlers, false beggars and vagrants, fined, outlawed, arrested, put in stocks or branded on the forehead with the letter F, for falsity. They are not even allowed to dress as they please – ploughmen must be content with blanket and russet cloth and common ladies with lambskin or rabbit.

Meanwhile the so-called 'Commons' in Parliament have voted to extend taxes to every man and woman in the land. The first Poll Tax, raised just four years ago, demanded a groat (four pence) from everyone over 14 to fund Edward III's everlasting war with France. Only the mendicant priests and long-standing paupers were spared. But that money, squeezed from those who needed it most, was quickly squandered on the battlefield. Two years later the Commons brought in a new tax – although this time they had the good sense to spread the burden a little more fairly, with rates depending on status. But if you think £22,000 was enough to sustain an army for more than a few months, you would be wrong. And so, last December, 1380, the poll tax returned, thrice as harsh as before. Now the sum required was 12 pence – a month's wages for the ordinary ploughman. Every township was to calculate the total it owed and then divide the burden so that the richest paid up to 60 groats and the poorest at least one groat.

At least, that was the theory. The returns revealed that a third of the taxable population had suddenly disappeared. So on 16 March Sir Robert Hales earned his nickname of 'Hob the Robber' by commissioning investigation squads to ravage the counties of Essex, Kent and Norfolk. The most famous of these squads was led by John Legg, a sergeant to the King. Legg's methods were grim but efficient. Each girl who claimed to fall below the age of 14 was forced to line up to be tested. One by one the investigators lifted up their skirts and checked whether they retained their virginity or not. More often than not their fathers would offer to pay up rather than subject them to public shame.

No wonder that the air is thick with dissent. The nobles can sense it too, or have read it for themselves in the poem *Piers Plowman*: 'Therefore I warn you rich, have ruth on poor folk; though you are mighty in the moot hall, be meek in your judgements, for the measure that you mete shall be meted to you; your weighs shall weight you when the hour is ready.' All the peasants need is a leader, someone who can persuade them to make a stand, and win. The Archbishop took steps to ensure John Ball could not play the part by seizing him from his home in Colchester and locking him up in this prison, but the 'Mad Priest of Kent' seems confident of his release. No doubt the cryptic letters play a part:

> Jack Carter prays to you all that you make a good end to what you have begun. Do well and ever better and better. Only in the evening can men praise the day. If the end be well, then all is well. Let Piers Plowman my brother dwell at home and prepare our food. I will go with you and help to prepare your meat and drink so that none of you fail. See that Hob the Robber be well chastized for losing your good opinion. You have great need to take God with you in all your deeds. For now is the time.

It as if John Ball is giving the coded signal to his followers – *now is the time*.

* * *

What is that trembling, that rumbling in the distance like thunder, that quaking of the earth with foot-sized raindrops? The noise grows ever loader – a shrieking unlike anything ever heard, so strange that it can only be compared to the mating cry of a peacock. The guards outside the cell mutter nervously as the walls shake before hurrying away to investigate. The din grows louder and individual voices can be heard. A few moments later and the door leading to the dungeon bangs against the wall as it is flung open. A face appears at the cell door. Keys are produced, the lock is sprung, and we are confronted by a small band of men armed with cudgels, bows and scythes. They have come to release John Ball. Out we go through the main gate, while others scurry past us carrying great piles of parchment – legal records destined for the bonfire. Before us a great chaotic mass of Kentish countrymen. These are not soldiers dressed for battle. They are peasants, craftsmen, small merchants, artisans and lowly priests. Many are barely out of childhood, others are fathers and grandfathers. Their swords and axes are rusty, their bows are blackened with age and smoke, their arrows bent or badly-plumed. But what they lack in equipment, they more than make up for in numbers. And the word is there are more on the way, from the furthest reaches of Kent, from Suffolk and Norfolk, from Essex, from Hertfordshire. There are rumours of 50,000, 100,000, even 200,000.

At the head of this advance force stands Wat Tyler, a former soldier himself, veteran of old Edward's war. He has enough presence to fill a field by himself. Even the nobility admit to his cunning and wit, his skill in public speaking and negotiation. The best insult they can throw at him is that he lacks charm and grace, just because he does not display the fawning courtesy that is expected of a lowborn 'bare-legged ruffian'. But this common citizen of Colchester has taken just a few days to demand the full attention of young King Richard and his advisers. The rebellion appears to have been brewing for a long time, waiting for the right moment to bubble over. That moment arrived on 1 June, when the townsmen of Fobbing in Essex refused to provide the further tax demanded. Thomas Bampton, the lord's steward, fled in disgrace upon his horse towards London rather than risk his head being impaled upon a spike.

The next day, vastly underestimating the breadth of support across the county, the Chief Justice of the Common Bench arrived with twenty soldiers on a commission of trailbaston to punish the rebels. Sir Robert Bealknapp arrived to find not only the townsmen of Fobbing but those of surrounding settlements armed and ready to lay down their lives. The whimpering knight was branded a traitor and forced to swear on the Bible that he would give up his commission. The jurors he had pressed into service for his inquest were tracked down, their houses burned down and their heads removed from their necks. Two days after that the rebels entered Colchester on their way to London. Meanwhile Tyler crossed the river to join a second force from Kent and release John Ball, the man whose preachings have inspired this great rising.

Before heading on to London Tyler sends a message to the king. 'We come not as thieves and robbers. We have risen to save the king from traitors and to free the people from slavery and injustice.' These peasants are the same soldiers, he says, whose arrows cut down the French. Surely they deserve their freedom?

* * *

Thirty miles down the road, at Greenwich on the Feast of Corpus Christi, 13 June 1381, we wait with countless thousands for a sight of the King. He should be easy to spot, this handsome lanky boy of 14 in an ill-fitting crown, even if he was not surrounded by courtiers and preceded by banners and flags. The rumour is that Richard will listen to Tyler's demands from his barge upon the Thames. Some say that he will not come. Others claim that he came yesterday but fled in terror at the sight of so many rebels. Still, we line the banks in expectation, fired up with the words of John Ball in his sermon in Blackheath that morning.

The priest began as he always did, with the saying that has become the unofficial slogan of the revolt: 'When Adam delved and eve span, who was then a gentleman.' Meaning, we were all created equal by nature and our servitude is an unjust and oppressive creation of man, not God. Otherwise God would have created a lord and a serf in the beginning. Instead we should all live as equals and share the bounties of the land. 'We are all Christ's creatures – therefore love each other like brothers and each give what he can spare as his goods are needed. Let each man help the other, for we shall all go hence.' But this time, his words were threaded with steel. 'Let us go to the king. He is young, and we will show him our miserable slavery, we will tell him it must be changed, or else we will provide the remedy ourselves. When the king sees us, either he will listen to us, or we will help ourselves.' And with a final roar: 'With King Richard and the True Commons.'

The minutes pass. Then a rumble of confirmation – is that the King? As the barge draws closer, flanked by a further four, we can make out a boy in deep conversation with his advisors, his Treasurer Hob the Robber, and the Archbishop of Canterbury Simon Sudbury. The very people most to blame for the sufferings of the people. The crowd is restless. Not until Richard has stepped ashore to talk with their leader Wat Tyler will they be satisfied.

Now the barge slows and stops. An exchange with someone on the bank, too far away for anything to be heard. And then, with no explanation, the King's barge turns and makes its way back up the river towards the Tower of London. A great roar of frustration erupts from the crowd. What now? We begin to move, first hesitantly and then in a great flood towards Southwark and London Bridge. Word spreads that we are heading into the city, although none know where exactly. Some say the Marshalsea and King's Bench Prisons in Southwark. Others say the prison at Newgate, or Hob the Robber's houses in Clerkenwell and Highbury. All that we do know is that we are not to steal anything – for Tyler has vowed to execute any who resort to theft or robbery.

By the time the surge carries us to Southwark the prisons have already been broken and the prisoners set free. Brothels frequented by the Mayor of London and the aristocracy have been set on fire. All too soon we are at the Bridge, which we are surprised to find untouched and open for our passage into the city. The noise is overwhelming as we surge on in a sweaty human mass to the other side of the river. And then the shouting grows even louder as groups split off – some north towards Aldgate, some west towards Ludgate and some east towards the Tower. We find ourselves drawn west, up towards Newgate and Fleet prisons, where convicts are emerging blinking into the light. Everywhere is chaos and noise. A marshal's house burns here, a chandler's shop there. At Temple the road is littered with the shards of roof tiles thrown down from above. There are bonfires of law books and court rolls. The smoke irritates our eyes and stings our throat.

By the time we reach the Strand, that ancient highway between the City and Westminster, we are exhausted and out of breath. Still we keep going – for up ahead we see the rebels taking on the finest house in London, the Savoy Palace, home to the King's uncle, the Duke of Lancaster John of Gaunt, a man whose name cannot fail to bring forth a stream of curses from even the most innocent young girl. This place, one of the finest monuments to greed and corruption in England, is ringed with huge walls and cost £35,000 to build – enough to fund the whole army for more than four months. Previously passers-by could only guess on what luxuries lay inside. Now the guards have been slain and the gates forced open to reveal a vast hidden interior: a great hall, a chapel, thatched cottages, stables, even a fishpond. Small groups of rebels stream back and forth between the buildings with lighted torches, setting everything to flame. An explosion goes off somewhere, like gunpowder. Who knows what fineries are going up in smoke – a wardrobe sufficient to clothe the entire aristocracy of England, the finest bed linen, ornate headboards, enough silver to fill five carts, more jewels than stars in the sky.

We hear later that one of the rebels tried to steal a large silver plate from the Duke's own apartments. He was seized by Tyler's men and flung on to the large fire already consuming the palace.

* * *

Justice of a different kind is dispensed the next day on Tower Hill. Before a scarcely believing crowd of rebels the Lord Chancellor himself, Simon of Sudbury, Archbishop of Canterbury, former Bishop of London and chaplain to Pope Innocent VI, is led out in chains. And not just him – all the most hated men of England are with him: Hob the Robber, John Legg and William Appleton, the chief adviser to John of Gaunt. These men, who have brought so much misery to the people of this land, are now to face their final reckoning at the hands of a peasant chosen from among our number, John Starling of Colchester. The Lord Chancellor is the first to expose his neck upon the block. No doubt he hopes the end will be swift.

We all rub our eyes and pinch our forearms, but this is no dream. Unexpected, yes. For we have heard it took only 400 men to storm the Tower. If the guards put up any resistance at all, we have seen no evidence. By all accounts the rebels simply walked in, greeting the soldiers as their own brothers and urging them to join the cause. Some say that King Richard gave his permission for these traitors to be executed. Whatever the truth, it was a surprise to all – the King's mother, fair maid of Kent, opened the door of the Royal Bedroom to find it occupied by swineherds and ploughmen. Naturally they requested the pleasure of a kiss, but the lady was not for kissing, only screaming. Not that she was ever in danger. Their target was Sudbury, the man who excommunicated, arrested and imprisoned John Ball. The man whose life is about to end.

Give him credit, he knows how to compose himself for an execution. Not like Sir Robert Hales, screaming for mercy and crying like a baby. Or John Legg, passed out from fear. No, it is only when the first blow lands, awkwardly, that Sudbury cries out: 'Ah, ah, this is the Hand of God.' His own hand instinctively goes to the gash in his neck just as the second blow lands, cutting off the tops of his fingers. But the head is still attached to the body. On the third blow the crowd begins to wince as well as cheer – this is bloody work. A fourth, a fifth, a sixth, and still the bone resists. It is only on the eighth that the Archbishop's head tumbles to the ground. A great roar greets the sight, and then another as the head is raised aloft. Three more heads, three more roars. All four will now be impaled upon spears and carried through the cheering crowds to London Bridge. There, as befitting their status as traitors, the heads will be publicly displayed, a reminder of this famous day.

* * *

It was only late that night we heard of another stunning success to rival that at the Tower. While we were witnessing the execution of the traitors, the King met the rebels gathered in Mile End. And, incredibly, agreed to their demands. Freedom from serfdom, freedom to trade and a free pardon. Cheap land available to rent at 4d an acre. Charters are to be drawn up, signed and distributed among every village and township, whether it be in Essex, Kent, Sussex, Bedford, Cambridge, Stafford or Lincoln. Many of the rebels decided to head home with their spoils, satisfied with the King's word. They had been away from their beds for nearly two weeks now. They were tired, their passions spent. And they had won their freedom.

So why are we still here, sweating at Smithfield with a few

thousand men? The King has asked to meet us here, or rather he has asked to meet Wat Tyler, the leader of this rising. Tyler will restate the demands that must be met before we return home: an end to serfdom and villeinage, free hunting and fishing, the land divided equally between all men, the church to give up its possessions, and a restoration of the old Anglo-Saxon law of Winchester. So it is that Tyler and a small number of his men ride across the field towards the King in front of St Bartholomew's leaving the rest of us, John Ball included, to nervously await the result. Nobody seems to know what is happening – the view is obscured, or it is too far away. Some suspect a trick – this is after all a famous execution site, the place where the brave Scottish heart of William Wallace was silenced three quarters of a century ago. But most have faith in the young King. Word even spreads that Richard has knighted Tyler – was that a swordflash in the sun? The crowd is unsure, nothing is clear. There are rumbles of confusion, and the nervous fingering of bowstrings. Will Tyler signal if he is in trouble? Should we go to him now, or stay here?

And then a whispering, the King, the King is coming. Straining for a view we can just make out a figure approaching swiftly on horseback. It is Richard himself, and alone. He is urging us to follow him north to Clerkenwell. What of Tyler? Will he meet us there? Nobody is sure. But we follow the King, *With King Richard and the True Commons*.

It is only when we reach St John's fields that we realise our trust has been misplaced all along. King Richard has led us directly into a trap, a trap lined with 8,000 men from the London militia led by Sir Robert Knolles, the knight famed for his exploits with King Edward in France. Knolles, even at 56, is not a man to tolerate dissent. 'Fall out you wretches! Slack your bowstrings and be gone!' We are surrounded 'like sheep in a fold'.

Tyler is dead, we are told. As for the charters and the promises of freedom, they are but worthless pieces of paper. Then the confirmation; Tyler's severed head is brought before us, set on a pole. It is clear now: Tyler is dead, and with him the rebellion.

There are several versions of Tyler's death. Some say he was killed after acting rudely and arrogantly in front of the King, either by spitting out water, tossing a knife from hand to hand, refusing to remove his cap, addressing the King as 'brother', demanding to hold the King's sword or taking the reins of the King's horse in his hand. It is also suggested he was provoked into attacking or threatening a member of the King's party before being cut down by the Mayor of London.

After Tyler's death the other rebel leaders were hunted down and executed and the revolt, which had spread as far north as Scarborough, Beverley and York, was suppressed. John Ball went on the run but was eventually found hiding in an old house in Coventry on 13 July 1381. He was charged with inciting rebellion and writing seditious letters and was sentenced to be hanged, drawn and quartered. His execution took place outside St Alban's abbey in Hertfordshire.

The Great Rising did perhaps bring one benefit, however – the hated Poll Tax did not return until the seventeenth century under Charles II.

CHAPTER 6

To the Spital House

In which we seek shelter at a hospital for the poor in York in November 1535, a few months before the dissolution of the monasteries by Henry VIII

The storm hits as we cover the last mile of the road towards York. Cold rain, driven into our faces by a bitter north wind, forces us to scramble under the porch of a spital house not far short of the Micklegate, the southern entrance to the city. There we stand, half-drowned and almost frozen, watching the black clouds grumble overhead as if threatening to hurl down hailstones as a big as the King's fist. The porter of the house seems glad of the company and the chance to unfurl his reminiscences of weather in all its divine manifestations. He is still midway through his recollection of a lightning strike when we notice a crowd of people gathering at the gate. One of them steps closer, a barefooted man with a scabby, pockmarked face and a back as crooked as his wooden staff.

'Good master, for your mother's blessing, give us a half penny toward our lodging?' he croaks. The rest of the group, some of them only boys, look on expectantly as their tattered clothing flaps in the wind.

The porter intervenes: 'What do you need to crave for? You shall have your lodging in the spital, and the sisters shall take care of you.'

The crooked man staggers away, but others continue to seek admission.

We ask the porter: 'Do you take in everybody who asks for lodging?'

He nods. 'We do, for the Lord's sake. They are those who cannot work or beg, or have no friends to support them. The elderly and the sick. Poor women heavy with child. Poor scholars loitering for crust and crumb. Wounded men, maimed soldiers and adventurers. Lepers and others afflicted by pestilence. There are even gentlemen and women who have fallen in great poverty through illness or other misfortune. We take them all in for a night or two, and if they die within our walls they are buried well and honestly.'

There are well over a dozen spital houses in York, including the oldest and largest, St Leonard's, to the north, across the River Ouse. It is said to date from before the Conquest and in the thirteenth century sheltered more than 200 people and distributed 247 loaves, 247 herrings, 33 dishes of meat and 13 gallons of ale at the gates every week. It had a guest house, school, nursery and infirmary staffed by thirteen monks, four priests, eight sisters and two schoolmasters, all of which is paid for by wealthy benefactors in return for the prayers of the inhabitants, known as 'beadsmen'. There were also 'cremetts', those poor who cannot work because they are blind, or lame, or bedridden, and corrodies, who have paid a fee to ensure they will be looked after in retirement. These days the hospital seems to be in decline – we are told there are now only around fifty residents.

On top of that there are the monasteries (three) and the priories (two), and the convent only a few hundred yards away to the east. All of which gives the city the air of being stuck in the Middle Ages; a victim of neglect by the Tudor kings who seized the throne from the House of York fifty years ago. You only have to look at the castle, with its ruined towers and arches, for evidence of its decline. Yet it is still the sixth largest city in England, with a population of 8,000, and many still rank it as second in importance behind London, as befits its status as the capital of the North.

Worse is on the way, it seems. There are rumours of new taxes to fund the king's love of gold, feasting and pageantry (and his queen Anne Boleyn too – although many would dispute that title). This year's harvest was the worst yet and wheat prices are 80 per cent higher than the previous year. Small farms are merging together into bigger farms,

47

the common land is being enclosed, and peasants are being forced to take to the road. Some fear a great horde of beggars set loose upon the country. Some say it is already bad enough, that the land is already plagued by these 'masterless men'; former soldiers and labourers who have lost their wage and turned to begging and stealing to survive. There are women too, adds the porter: 'They come so thick that they stop the way – the sisterhood of drabbes, sluttes and callets, with their bags and wallets.'

The increase in the numbers of the poor has been remarked upon by the writer Simon Fish, who described in a letter to the King the 'wretched hideous monsters, the foul unhappy sort of lepers, and other sore people, needy, impotent, blind, lame, and sick, that live only by alms'. In his eyes the counterfeit beggars are the bishops, abbots, deacons and monks of the Catholic Church who own more than a third of the land and claim a tenth part of everything produced by the people. Henry VIII responded in 1531 with the statute for the punishment of vagabonds and beggars, who 'daily do increase in great and excessive numbers by the occasion of idleness, mother and root of all vices' and are responsible for 'thefts, murders and other heinous offences and great enormities to the high displeasure of God'.

We hear tales of idlers and thieves feigning illness and infirmity to take advantage of our charity. They are called 'mighty beggars' and many more names besides: hedgecreepers, fylloks and lustes, trewands and vagabonds. They do not work but prefer to wander from place to place. In summer they hunt blackberries and in winter they flock into town looking for hospitality, or sleep in porches and in doors, in hay lofts or sheep-cotes.

The porter knows their type: 'They go about with bloody clothes and plasters on their skin,' he says. 'Some feign leprosy. Others put soap in their mouths to make it foam and fall down as if they have Saint Cornelius' evil. But when they are in their own company they are as fit as you or I.'

There are laws against such things already. Forty years ago Henry VII ordered that all 'idle vagabonds' in towns and cities should be put in the stocks for three days and three nights before being sent away to their birthplace. If they returned they would be put in the stocks for six days. Anyone who fed them with anything other than bread and water was fined twelve pence. In York, as in London, the authorities attempted to license beggars by giving them tokens. Only those with tokens were allowed to ask for alms. The others were to be cast out. Five years ago Henry VIII passed another law ordering all unlicensed and able-bodied beggars to be stripped naked and whipped until their bodies ran with blood. Even harsher punishments are reserved for those who attempt to deceive the public with disguises or by claiming to be 'doctors of physic', fortune tellers or gypsies: they will be whipped for two days for a first offence, have one ear cut off for a second offence and the remaining ear cut off for a third offence.

In 1536 The Suppression of Religious Houses Act allowed Henry VIII to seize all religious houses valued at less than £200 a year (the remaining 552 houses followed in 1539). In May 1536 Anne Boleyn was beheaded. In October that year, the city of York was occupied by rebels during the 'Pilgrimage of Grace', which was inspired partly by the dissolution of the monasteries and partly by economic grievances (letters were sent out across the north of England in the name of 'Captain Poverty'). The revolt failed and its leader Robert Aske was hung in chains from Clifford's Tower in York in July 1537.

CHAPTER 7

The Counterfeit Crank

*In which we meet the notorious idle beggar Nicholas Genings,
alias Nicolas Blunt, in 1566/7 and note the changes in
the treatment of vagrants over the last 30 years*

Is this a man or a monster? Or a zombie creature summoned forth by a gypsy curse? He staggers and stumbles towards us, almost naked but for a patchwork of rags covering what little modesty still remains. A tattered leather jerkin hangs open to reveal a bare chest streaked with dirt. The sackcloth scraps that pose for hose leggings look as if they might fall to pieces at any moment. His face is even uglier to behold, framed by a filthy headcloth draping down either side of his face. His cheeks are smeared with blood and white foaming drool drips from his mouth down his trussed-up beard. And the smell! So noxious that anyone would be only too happy to throw in a penny to send him on his way – which perhaps explains why he is clutching an old felt hat in one hand like a collection dish ready to receive our charity.

'Ah good master,' he greets us in a low murmur, his eyes cast down at the ground. 'I have the grievous and painful disease called the falling sickness and I can get no remedy for the same, for my father had it, and my friends before me.'

'How come your jerkin, hose and hat are so dirty, and your skin,' we ask.

'Ah, I fell down on the backside here in a foul lane hard by the waterside and lay almost all night and bled almost all the blood out in my body.'

We offer to take him somewhere to wash himself, but he refuses even to bathe in the tub of rain water nearby.

'If I should wash myself I should fall to bleeding afresh again and then I should not stop myself,' he says.

The beggar tells us his name is Nicholas Genings. He was born at Leicester but has roamed around the country since. Two years ago he moved from Dartford in Kent to London where it is felt that charity is easier to come by. He says he has spent the last eighteen months in Bethlehem Hospital just outside the walls near Bishopsgate. Today he is begging in Newington, south of the river.

We are about to ask him more about his trade when a gentleman appears with a constable to accuse Genings of being a 'Counterfeit Crank'. It is rumoured that there are scores of these hideous charlatans plying the streets in increasingly convincing disguises. So successful is the ruse, it is claimed, that they earn far more in a day than an honest working man does in a week.

Genings protests his case. 'I have but twelve pence,' he says, holding out his hat. 'I have no more, as god shall save my soul at the day of judgement'.

The constable is not satisfied, and searches through Genings' rags (a task we do not envy him for), before pulling out a purse. It contains another 40 pence.

'I pray to God I will be damned both body and soul if I have any more,' he vows, but the constable is still not satisfied. Another purse appears -- this time containing eight shillings.

Genings looks beaten – his game is up. The constable strips the rags from his body, unties his beard and scrubs him down with rainwater from the tub. The blood and the dirt runs off leaving no trace of injury or disease. Genings now looks positively handsome, with his flaxen yellow beard and his healthy white skin glowing in the dusky light. Shamefaced, the Counterfeit Crank asks for a cloak to cover himself. The constable reluctantly agrees, ushers him into a nearby inn and calls for a pot of beer. Genings drinks it down in one go and calls for another, and then a third, perhaps fearful of where he will end up tonight. All done, he begs permission to go and 'make water' and is led to the back yard.

The gentleman who summoned the constable is Thomas Harman,

a landowner from Kent who now lodges in the cloister of Whitefriars. It seems he first met Genings on All Hallow's Day of this year, 1566, and was immediately suspected his true nature. 'The Crank approached three great ladies, lamenting and crying to be relieved,' says Harman. 'I heard his doleful words and rueful mournings, hearing him name the fallen sickness, just as you did.'

Harman then checked with Bethlehem Hospital and discovered that nobody of his name had ever laid there. Two servant boys were sent to find Genings and keep him under observation.

'They found the same Crank begging about the Temple,' says Harman. 'At about twelve o'clock he went on the back-side of Clement's Inn without Temple Bar where there is a lane that goeth into the fields. There he renewed his face again with fresh blood which he carried about him in a bladder, and daubed fresh dirt upon his jerkin, hat and hosen. And so he came back again to the Temple and begged of all that passed by – some gave groats, some sixpence, some gave more, for he looked so ugly and irksomely that everyone pitied his miserable case.'

'And the foaming mouth?' we ask.

'Nothing more than a piece of white soap upon which he chews.'

Suddenly we hear a shout. We look around to see Genings running stark naked across the fields. The constable attempts to chase after him, but soon gives up. Darkness is falling and the Crank quickly fades into the distance.

Harman tells us that Genings' real name is Nicholas Blunt, whose other guise (when he is not turned Crank) is the 'upright man'. But what is an upright man?

'Some of them are serving men, artificers and labouring men, who will wander through the wealthiest shires of this realm, from Somerset to Norfolk, to claim relief even though they risk the stocks or a whipping. The upright man will not ask for forgiveness until he is on the gallows. He will accept only money – if he is offered meat or drink he will scornfully refuse, and if he sees any pigs or chickens about he will remember the place and return to steal them the next night.'

And what does he do with his ill-gotten gains?

'Why, he repairs to tippling houses with harlots, who are also skilful in picking, rifling and filching. They spend their evenings boozing belly cheer to one another and at night they sleep together in barns as dog and bitch.' He explains how the Doxy fashions a bed out of straw or hay covered with a petticoat or a cloak and a pillow out of a wallet or a bundle of rags. If it is warm they take off their smocks, but if it is cold they lie in their smocks and cover themselves with hay or straw. Then the Upright Man enters and takes his choice of Doxy. 'But you won't see an upright man walking with his Doxy by day,' he says. 'They go separate for a month at a time, only meeting at fairs or markets to steal from the stalls before retiring to the woods to spend three or four days having their fill of meat and drink.'

When we ask how he comes to know their habits in such detail, he replies: 'I have been accustomed to talk and confer daily with many of these wily wanderers, of both sorts, as well men and women, boys and girls,' he confirms. 'If you wish, I can acquaint you with the abominable, wicked and detestable behaviour of all these rowsey, ragged rabblement of rake-hells, that under the pretence of great misery, diseases and other innumerable calamities, which they feign through great hypocrisy, do win and gain great alms in all places.'

Harman leads us a short way along the road before spotting a woman begging from passers-by. 'Here is a Walking Mort,' he tells us sternly, before reprimanding her for her 'lewd life and beastly behaviour' and warning her she would be punished for her 'filthy living and wretched conversation'.

The Walking Mort replies, apparently without taking offence: 'God help how I should live, none will take me into service but I labour in harvest time honestly.' She then launches into a story about how she travelled to the Kent Coast while pregnant so she could gorge on mussels and oysters, only to get stuck in a hole in the rocks. When she is done, she agrees to lead us to a tippling house where we may observe a company of vagabonds plotting their next escapades. Soon we are occupying a table on the other side of the room from a group of men and women laughing and drinking. While some appear feeble, others are as hardy as the labourer in the field. We nod towards one of the strongest, and seek an explanation.

'He is a Ruffler,' says Harman. 'He is the first in degree of this odious order, a soldier or a serving man who chooses the idle life over hard work and wanders about demanding charity, claiming he has been maimed fighting for his country. If he shows you a wound or a bruise it has no doubt been earned in a drunken fight. And if begging fails they will steal from women or old men riding to market, and even from other beggars.'

Another man, dressed in a frieze jerkin and gally slops (baggy hose reaching just below the knee), holds a long wooden staff with an iron hook mounted on the end. 'The Angler,' he explains. 'They practise pilfering by night, as during the day they go house to house demanding charity, marking out prey, noting apparel, linen etc.' Later in the night they return with their fishing pole to reach through open windows and pluck out everything of value within reach. 'I have heard a tale of an angler so audacious he plucked the bed covers from a farmer and his two sons as they slept, leaving them lying naked but for their shirts,' says Harman.

Next to the Angler is the Rogue, who is weaker than the upright man and walks about with a stick, feigning infirmity and begging for pennies. Some of them, the ones Harman calls Wild Rogues, threaten to beat a man's brains out unless they hand over their entire purses, before fleeing over the hedgerows. 'I once rebuked a wild rogue for wandering idly about and he told me that he was a beggar by inheritance,' says Harman. 'His grandfather was a beggar, his father was one and he must be one by good reason.'

Opposite the Rogue is a lewdly dressed woman of indeterminate years, whose former good looks have been ruined by only six or seven years on the road. 'She is a Doxy,' Harman tells us. 'They are broken and spoiled of their maidenhead by the Upright Men. And afterward she is common and indifferent for any that will use her.' He tells of one Doxy who was familiar with at least seven Upright Men who were all hanged for vagrancy. 'There is one notorious harlot of this affinity called Besse Bottomely,' adds Harman. 'She hath but one hand, and she hath murdered two children at least.'

Harman explains that a young woman who has not yet been broken by the Upright Man is known as a Dell.

'How does a woman end up as a Dell?' we ask.

'Either by the death of their parents or nobody to look after them, or else they flee the service of a sharp Mistress. Some are born into it with their monstrous mothers, and must of necessity be as evil or worse than their parents.' Even younger than the Dell is the Kinchin Mort, a girl still small enough to be carried on the backs of her vagrant mother, wrapped in a sheet.

Perched on a stool alongside the Doxy is a rough-looking sailor with an Irish accent. 'I call him a whip-jack, or a freshwater mariner,' says Harman. These men falsely claim their ship has been wrecked or attacked by pirates, often with counterfeit begging licences to prove it. 'Sometimes they counterfeit the seal of the Admiralty,' Harman explains. 'I have divers times confiscated their licences with such money as they have gathered. Once I asked who made their licences and they swore that they bought it from a mariner at Portsmouth for two shillings.'

Next to the whipjack is a younger man in a leather jerkin with a little wand clutched in his hand. 'The Prigger of Prancers,' we are informed, otherwise known as a horse-stealer. His kind will pretend to watch over a gentleman's horses in return for a penny but will ride off on them if left alone for even a second.

Harman then points to a hideous beggar whose skin is everywhere defaced with blisters and sores. 'A Palliard,' says Harman, explaining that they raise the blisters by rubbing ratsbane or spearwort over their bodies. Most of them are Welshmen,' he adds.

We then attempt to eavesdrop upon their conversation, but have difficulty understanding their strange language, called 'Canting' or 'Pedlar's French'.

'This bowse is as good as Rome bowse,' slurs the Whipjack, quaffing his drink.

'I'll couch a hogshead in a skipper this darkemans', says the Doxy.

'No, now we have well bowsed, let us strike some chete,' replies the Rogue, mentioning an old lady's farm nearby. 'She hath a cackling chete, a grunting chete, ruff pecke, cassan and poppelars of yarum.'

Harman translates. The Doxy wishes to sleep in a barn tonight, but the Rogue prefers to go stealing ('strike some chete'), having drunk ('bowsed') his fill of ale. Apparently the old lady has a hen, a pig, bacon, cheese and milk porridge available for pilfering.

Finally, we are given a description of Bawdy Baskets, Abraham Men and Dummerers. The first are women who pester servant girls on doorsteps to exchange cheap laces, silk girdles, pins and needles for more expensive beef, bacon or cheese. Abraham Men feign madness and sing and dance on your doorstep for money, bacon, cheese or wool, while Dummerers double up their tongues and groan and moan while cupping their hands for money. 'These Dummerers are lewd and most subtle people, and will never speak unless they have extreme punishment,' says Harman, before bidding us goodnight. Another time he may show us drunken tinkers, swaddlers, jarke men and demanders of glimmers, and tell us the story of the cuffin (man), the bufe (dog) and the jockam (penis).

'Bene lightmans to thy quaromes,' we reply, wishing him a good morrow.

* * *

On 13 January 1567 the Counterfeit Crank appears before the Court of Aldermen in the City of London, presided over by the Lord Mayor. The charge is that he 'divers and sundry times heretofore used and counterfeited himself to be a diseased person with the grievous disease of the falling sickness and hath also of a set purpose disfigured his body with dire loathsome spots and other filthiness in his face and other parts of his body to the only intent to be thereby permitted to begge and to delude as he hath already a long time done the good and charitable people.' Genings has been going around the city claiming to be a poor unemployed hatmaker, begging for a few pennies for his night's lodging before he seeks work the following morning. He was spotted by Thomas Harman in Ludgate and chased as far as the Fleet

Bridge before being arrested. When his home in Master's Hill Rents was searched, it was revealed to be 'a pretty house well stuffed with a fair joint table and a fair cupboard garnished with pewter'.

Genings is sentenced to be tied naked to the tail of a cart and whipped through the common market places of the city while carrying a picture of himself as the Counterfeit Crank. He will then be committed to Bridewell Prison to work away his idle nature.

Perhaps he is lucky to escape more serious punishment. We have heard how in 1531 the punishments ranged from being whipped to having an ear chopped off. Sixteen years later Edward VI tried to crack down on idle beggars even more harshly – by turning them into slaves. Under that statute every able person who turned down honest work faced being marked on the breast with a hot iron in the shape of a V for vagabond and banished back to their birthplaces with a certificate such as this:

A.B., Justice of the Peace in the county of S, to the Mayor or Chief Officer of the city of C, greetings:

According to a most godly statute made in the first year of the reign of our sovereign lord King Edward the Sixth. we have taken this bearer I.L. vagrantly and to the evil example of others without master, service or labour whereby to get his living going loitering idly about, and because the same saith he was born in C in the countie of S, whereof you are the head officer we have sent him to you to be ordered according to the purporte and effect of the same statute, and with this writing shall deliver the same loiterer to the constables or other head officer of the said city, there to be nourished and kept in chains either at the common works in amending highways or other common work or from man to man in order til they which may bear be equally charged, to be slave to the corporation of the city or to the inhabitants of the town or village, upon pain that for every such default that the said slave doth live idly by the defaults of the city by the space of three working days together the city to forfeit five pounds.

The slave could be put to labour, willingly or willingly, and sustained on bread, water or scraps of meat not fit for the table. If the ungrateful slave attempted to run away his master was permitted to punish him with a beating, lock him up in chains and mark him on the forehead with a hot iron in the shape of an S. If he dared to run away a second time he would be sentenced to death. As for the children aged between five and 14, they could be taken by force and put to work as an apprentice or servant until the age of 24 for men and 20 for women. They too were slaves, liable to be let, sold or given away by their masters.

So severe was the punishment that it appears it was hardly, if ever, enacted, and the law was repealed within a few years. But the beggars continued to multiply, if you believe the account of Sir John Cheke, who claimed in 1549 at the time of Kett's Rebellion that they 'swarm in every corner of the realm and not only lie loitering under hedges but also stand in cities and beg boldly at every door. Valiant beggars play in towns and yet complain of need, contenting themselves better with idle beggary than with honest and profitable labour.'

Three years ago Queen Elizabeth ordered licensing of genuine beggars across the whole country and the punishment of the able-bodied poor who refused to work in husbandry. Not one of these measures appears to have worked. Perhaps there are other explanations besides idleness?

The Counterfeit Crank was released from Bridewell prison on condition he remained an honest man and earned his living by hard work instead of fakery. Did he keep his promise? His fate is unknown.

CHAPTER 8

A Census of the Poor

*In which we investigate the condition of poor in Norwich
in 1570 and assess their suitability for alms*

A disabled beggar is being questioned by the authorities in Norwich. His name is Edmonde Abbott, and his right arm hangs uselessly at his side.

'I desire your mastership to be good and friendly to a poor man who hath been hurt and maimed in the Queen's affairs,' says the beggar, pointing to his crippled limb, 'maimed in my arm as your mastership may well perceive.'

'How came it to pass?' asks the suspicious official.

'I was hurt with a piece of ordinance, if it may please your mastership.'

'Where did you serve?'

'I served in one of the Queen's galleys called Spedewell and was hurt being on the narrow seas.'

'How long since you were hurt?'

'I was hurt at Whitsuntide, was 12 month.'

'Who was then captain of that galley?'

'Captain Holden.'

'In what conflict were you hurt?'

'I was hurt between Portsmouth and the Isle of Wight being matched and coupled with one of the French king's ships.'

The official, apparently satisfied, allows the beggar to go without punishment but insists on escorting him to the city gates. Norwich may be the second city of England and capital of one of the most prosperous counties, with a population of nearly 11,000, but it appears to have lost its patience with the men, women and children who go from door to door seeking money and food (not to mention the recent influx of Dutch and Walloon immigrants, but at least they appear to be hard workers). There are complaints of idlers rejecting hard work and choosing instead to lounge about in victualling houses, lying, swearing, drinking and fornicating out of wedlock. Rather than pay for their lodgings, they sleep in church porches, in doorways and dark corners, cellars, barns and hay chambers. Their flesh crawls with vermin. They spread disease. There are even stories of fussy beggars tossing away leftover pottage, bread, meat and drink, after stuffing themselves with the generosity of the citizens. Mayor John Aldrich claims they are costing the city more than £200 a year. So a census of the poor has been ordered, to decide who will be given alms, who will be put to work, and who will be cast outside the walls.

The census begins in the southernmost parish of St Peter of Southgate, on the west bank of the river that cuts the city in two. Here a family has been ordered to pack up and leave their rented room on the grounds that they have lived in Norwich less than three years. Richard Rich is a 35-year-old 'husbandman' or tenant farmer who occasionally lives with his wife Margaret and their four children – twelve-year-old Jone, eight-year-old Symond, four-year-old Alice and eight-month-old Fader. Like many other women in the city, Margaret and Jone try and earn a meagre living by spinning white warp into yarn by hand. It is clearly not enough, as the census taker marks them down in the book as 'Veri poor' but adds that they should receive no alms. Norwich has withdrawn its hospitality and suggests they return to the village of Banham twenty miles to the south-west.

Their near neighbours, the Browne family living in the south gatehouse, are receiving four pence a week in alms. Peter Browne, the porter, is a 50-year-old cobbler who struggles to get work to support his sick 60-year-old wife Agnes and their three daughters aged 14, 16 and 18. One of them lost their job as a servant to William Naught of Thorp and none of them have been able to find any spinning work recently. Also receiving alms of four pence a week is Anne Claxton and her two young sons. Although her husband Rafe is working out of town as a boatwright she has a mortgage to pay and is heavily pregnant. They are not exactly poor but at least they have lived in Norwich from birth.

As we move northwards along King Street towards the Norman castle keep the list of the poor grows longer: in one single house we find Alice Reade, a 40-year-old woman whose husband ran off leaving her to look after their four children; Robert Hemming, a 60-year-old husband and father lying bedbound with a hideous disease all over his body; and Margaret Palmer, a 48-year-old widow who spins wool and washes clothes. Only one person in the building receives anything, although we cannot discern why fortune should favour the widow Anne King and her 17-year-old daughter with one penny a week when others receive nothing.

The list of occupations noted down by the census taker includes bakers, tinkers, out-of-work sailors, labourers, tailors, masons, carpenters, bodgers, haymakers, cordwainers, embroiderers, weavers, glovers, hatmakers, blacksmiths, ostlers, bookbinders, bowers (dairymen) and slaughtermen. One man in the parish, 46-year-old John Browne, earns the title 'vagrant' but his family – his wife Jone and their four children – are awarded one penny a week. John Tomson is called a 'rogue of no occupation' and claims to have no idea where he originally lived before he came to Norwich and married a local girl called Tanyzen. It is perhaps this relationship which saves him from being expelled. There are many who are currently out of work. Some of them are disabled in one way or another: the lame, blind or dumb; Gefry Roberdes, a 56-year-old cobbler, is 'diseased with the stone'; the mason Anthony Smith is miserable with gout; 77-year-old Walter Holles 'all crooked'; John Tittle the hatter is simply 'very sick'. Others are simply too old. That doesn't stop Jone Forcet, who claims to be 100 years of age and still spins the white warp. She receives four pence a week in alms, whereas the city's other centenarian (and Jone's only competition for oldest citizen), Cicely Amis, is unable to work and receives no alms at all.

We now reach the castle and the parish of St Martin at the Bale, although the church itself was recently demolished and its bells and lead (valued at £76) donated to the Queen. Begging at the gates are Eme Stowe, an 80-year-old widow with a lame, withered arm, and her eleven-year-old grandson. There is no sign of the boy's mother or father; he is regarded as a 'bastard', born out of wedlock and it may be old Mrs Stowe had adopted him to increase her chances of getting alms. The census taker records that they are allotted two pence a week. Here also is the 'whore of Havergate' who touts for business at nine o'clock in the evening and is of 'much evil resort'. She is currently lazing about in bed, alone, but will no doubt soon be sent back to where she came from, a village twelve miles north of the city.

The census taker has been told to note down details of all such 'harlots' in the city. His list already includes eleven names: the 'gresse wenches' (local slang for those single women who are said to have lost their innocence upon the grass) Margoret Burches, Margoret Paterson and Elizabeth Rokes of St Peter per Montergate parish, Jane Abell, Alys Lane and Rose Fidemund from All Saint's parish just to the south of the castle; the widow Eliza Warde and Jone, of the parish of St John Maddermarket a few minutes' walk to the north-west; Margaret Cook in the parish of St Martin at Oak across the river; Elizabeth Gask and Mabel a Breton, a 23-year-old maidservant, in the parish of St Mary Unburnt (so-called because the church escaped a fire in the reign of William the Conqueror). How does the census taker know they are harlots? In most cases, it is because they are single mothers or unmarried and pregnant. They will either be sent away or put into service to change their ways. The census taker tells us of one young woman by the name of Benet Gedwyis, who eight years ago was convicted of 'whoredome' with a young glover in her master's garden. Aged 18, she was ordered to ride in a cart with a paper on her head before being tied to a ducking stool and plunged into the water. She was advised to give up her 'evyll life' and is now living with her two children aged one and five at the house of Edward Pye, Sheriff of Norwich, and spinning white warp to earn a living.

Next is the 'House of the Poor' or 'God's House' in Bishopsgate to the northeast of the Cathedral. Before the dissolution it was known as

St Giles' Hospital and distributed bread, meat, fish, eggs, cheese and drink to thirteen poor men every day of the year, either at the entrance during summer or by the fire in winter. It had thirty beds for the sick, who were cared for by three or four nuns. There was also a brewery. Twenty years ago it was the scene of one of the most notorious events in Norwich's history, the killing of Lord Sheffield during Kett's Rebellion of 1549, an uprising of disgruntled peasants against the enclosure of fields by wealthy landowners. It was this event that led to the city introducing a tax towards poor relief in 1550, ranging from a halfpenny a week for the middle-ranking citizen to one shilling and four pence a week for the likes of the Bishop of Norwich. And so Norwich became the first English city outside London to introduce a compulsory poor rate.

These days the hospital offers lodging, meat and drink for forty people, separated into wards of men and women. We meet William Hales and his wife, a couple in their eighties who are tended to by an 18-year-old maid and receive 12 pence a week in alms; cobbler John Myles, his wife Katherine and their five children (with one more on the way); and Florence Fakener, whose husband is a patient in the hospital, and their eleven-year-old daughter. The census taker has spotted one family to be sent away – John Furnell, a 70-year-old clerk and his wife Margery who have only recently arrived here from Plumstead, to the east of the city. A harlot named Alyce also goes down in the book.

Finally we reach 'The Normans', otherwise known as the Hospital of St Paul, in the north-eastern district of the city. The residents are mostly elderly or widowed women, such as lame Margaret West in house number five (the census taker calls her 'miserable pore'). She receives one-and-a-half pence in alms a week but her living companions, 88-year-old John Silie and his lame-handed wife Agnes receive nothing. But our interest is for once not in the current residents – it is in the building itself. For there are plans to turn the hospital into the centrepiece of Norwich's new scheme for the relief of the poor: a house of correction.

* * *

It is now June 1571 and begging has been banned inside the city walls. Anyone who does so is to be whipped six times and anyone who gives them money or food will be fined four pence a time. Only the genuinely sick and needy are to be maintained on alms. So-called 'strong beggars' are to be expelled, idle loiterers are to be set to work grinding malt or spinning wool in the bridewell and the young are to be placed into apprenticeships. The deacons are responsible for the poor in their wards and are to search once a month for any poor people who have not lived here for more than three years. A number of 'select women' have been chosen to look after up to twelve poor children and women a day; they teach the young to read and write and put the older maids to work until (in the words of the authorities) 'labour and learning shall be easier to them than idleness'. It is a full day of labour – from eight in the morning to four in the afternoon at winter and six in the morning to seven at night in the summer, with a two-hour break in the middle for dinner. If the children refuse to study then they will be sent to the bridewell and their parents face losing their weekly alms.

This new scheme is said to be saving the city £2,818 1s 4d a year by putting 950 idle children, 64 male beggars and 140 female beggars, to work. Has the vagabond problem been solved?

The scheme set up in Norwich influenced the 1572 Act for the punishment of vagabonds and for relief of the poor and impotent, which allowed all suspected rogues, vagabonds and sturdy beggars aged under 14 to be sent to gaol to await trial. If convicted they faced being whipped and burnt through the gristle of the right ear with a hot iron unless an 'honest person' took them into service. A second offence is punishable by the burning of the left ear, and a third means the death sentence. The same law also targets fortune tellers, wandering minstrels, jugglers, pedlars and tinkers. It appears to have been successful, as the historian John Stow reported that by 1575 rogues and masterless men in London had almost vanished from sight.

Peasants harvesting wheat with reaping-hooks, on a calendar page for August in the *Queen Mary Psalter*, c.1310. (British Library Illuminated Manuscripts Collection)

Peasants driving oxen and bulls, on a calendar page for April (zodiac sign Taurus) in the *Queen Mary Psalter*. (British Library Illuminated Manuscripts Collection)

St Francis making his plain brown habit. From *The Taymouth Hours*, early fourteenth century. (British Library Illuminated Manuscripts Collection)

Preacher John Ball (centre, on horseback) and the rebels led by Wat Tyler (front left). (British Library)

Illustration from *Hye-Waye to the Spyttel-House*, by Thomas Copland c. 1535. Standing from left to right are the porter, Copland and a beggar. (British Library)

The Beggars' Dole, painted glass depicting hungry beggars receiving food, from Rotha Mary Clay, *The Medieval Hospitals of England* (1909). (Wellcome Images Collection)

Print from Thomas Harman's *Caveat for Common Cursetors* (1566), showing the Counterfeit Crank Nicolas Genings (right) and his alter ego Nicolas Blunt, an Upright Man. (British Library)

Bridewell Prison in 1720, as rebuilt following the Great Fire of London. (Wellcome Images Collection)

Elizabeth Clarke and another witch identify their familiars under interrogation by Witchfinder-General Matthew Hopkins. Etching c.1792, after earlier woodcut. (Wellcome Images Collection)

A panorama of Bartholomew Fair in 1721, published by J. F. Setchel in Covent Garden, c.1800. (Wellcome Images Collection)

Print of Bartholomew Fair by Thomas Rowlandson, after the watercolour by John Nixon, c.1813. (Wellcome Images Collection)

New Bedlam at Moorfields, early eighteenth century engraving after Robert Hooke. (Wellcome Images Collection)

Scene from Bedlam in William Hogarth's *Rake's Progress* from 1731. Wealthy merchant's son Tom Rakewell loses his inheritance through gambling and is locked up in Fleet Debtor's Prison before ending up at Bethlehem Hospital. (Wellcome Images Collection).

The artist William Hogarth produced his famous depiction of 'Gin Lane' in 1751. In the foreground a diseased prostitute drops her infant child while under the influence of 'Mothers' Ruin'. This copy is an engraving by H. Adlard from *The Works of William Hogarth* (1833). (Author's collection).

The scene at Tyburn, as depicted by William Hogarth in the 'Idle Prentice', from the *Industry and Idleness* series of 1747.

A view of the Foundling Hospital, engraving by N. Parr after L. P. Boitard, 1753. (Wellcome Images Collection).

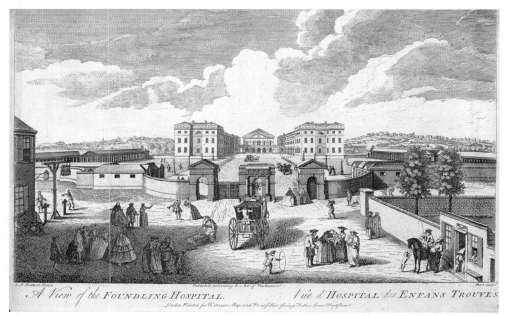

Young country girl Moll is seduced by a brothel keeper on arrival in London, in a scene from Hogarth's *Harlot's Progress*. (Wellcome Images Collection)

Bridewell Prison depicted in 1732 in William Hogarth's *Harlot's Progress*. The prostitute Moll, who arrived in London as a country girl seeking work as a seamstress, has been arrested and set to work beating hemp. (Wellcome Images Collection)

'A Woman of All Trades', showing a Covent Garden prostitute, printed in 1792. (Library of Congress)

Billy Waters, the well-known black busker and beggar of London. (Wellcome Images Collection)

Master Toby, a well-known imposter who pretended to be disabled to beg from passers-by in early nineteenth-century London. Engraving by Robert Cooper, 1822. (Wellcome Images Collection)

Street entertainer Joseph Johnson wore a model of the ship *Nelson* upon his cap while singing 'The Storm'. Etching by John Thomas Smith in 1815. (Wellcome Images Collection)

A spinning wheel and a stocking frame, in an etching by Thomas Jefferys. (Wellcome Images Collection)

Dinner at the Workhouse, from *Living London* by George Sims (1901). (Author's collection)

THE WALLFLOWER GIRL.
[From a Daguerreotype by Beard.]

Teenage girl selling flowers on the street, from Henry Mayhew's *London Labour and the London Poor* (1851). (Author's collection)

Crossing-sweeper boys pestering a gentleman for money, from *London Labour and the London Poor*. (Author's collection)

THE BOY CROSSING-SWEEPERS.
[From a Daguerreotype by Beard.]

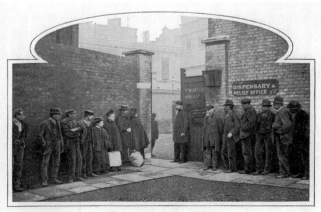

CASUALS WAITING FOR ADMISSION.

Casuals wait for admission to the workhouse, from *Living London*. (Author's collection)

A vagrant in 1846, from C. J. Ribton-Turner, *A History of Vagrants and Vagrancy, and Beggars and Begging* (1887). (Wellcome Images Collection)

Widow and child featured in 'The Crawlers', from John Thompson's *Street Life in London* (1877). (London School of Economics)

The homeless sleeping out in St James' Park in 1887, from *The Graphic*. (Author's collection)

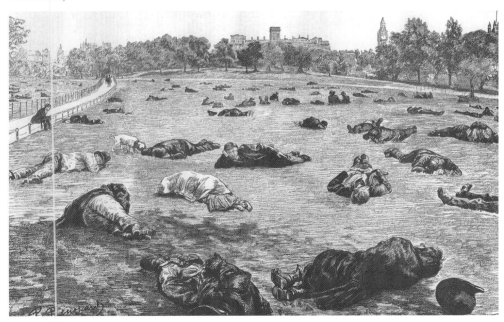

MAP DESCRIPTIVE OF LONDON POVERTY, 1898-9
(IN 12 SHEETS)

SHEET 5.
EAST CENTRAL DISTRICT

THE STREETS ARE COLOURED ACCORDING TO THE GENERAL CONDITION OF THE INHABITANTS, AS UNDER:—

Lowest class. Vicious, semi-criminal. | Very poor, casual. Chronic want. | Poor. 18s. to 21s. a week for a moderate family. | Mixed. Some comfortable, others poor. | Fairly comfortable. Good ordinary earnings. | Middle class. Well-to-do. | NIL | Upper-middle and Upper classes. Wealthy.

A combination of colours—as dark blue and black, or pink and red—indicates that the street contains a fair proportion of each of the classes represented by the respective colours.

A section of Charles Booth's poverty map of 1889–98, showing east London. The poorest sections were coloured black or dark blue, the middle class areas in bright red and the wealthiest in yellow. (London School of Economics)

Coffin-style beds were a common feature of casual wards and homeless shelters, including Medland Hall Refuge in east London, pictured in *Living London*. (Author's collection)

The alternative to the casual ward was paying a few pence for a bed at the many common lodging houses, such as this one in Spitalfields, from *Living London*. (Author's collection)

CHAPTER 9

Bridewell

*In which we visit the archetypal house of correction
known as Bridewell in London following the 1601 Act for
the Relief of the Poor, speak to the inmates there and
witness a whipping in front of the governors*

There is perhaps no stranger sight in London than Bridewell. Here a beggar can truly imagine what it is to be like to be a king, for this prison just north of the River Thames was once a palace. From the outside it looks the same as it did when it was built at a cost of £39,000 for Henry VIII – a wide, large red-brick house in the Tudor style with six turreted towers and heavy stone-framed windows. It is centrally located between the City and Westminster but quickly fell out of royal favour, perhaps because any visitor must pass through stinking lanes or over the filthy ditch known as the River Fleet to reach its gates.

So in 1553 the palace was handed over to the City of London and put to use as a home for the thriftless poor – 'the rioter that consumeth all; the vagabond that will abide in no place; the idle person, as dissolute women and others'. Its mission remains the same today. Of most concern to the authorities are the young vagrants hanging around the streets getting up to mischief of every kind imaginable: picking your pockets or pestering you for money, selling ballads and other pamphlets and generally doing anything except honest labour. It is these potential troublemakers who are sent to Bridewell to learn the meaning of hard work (and the feel of the lash upon their backs). This place will, in the language of the times, offer them 'opportunities for amendment of character'.

So it is with nervous glances that we cross the Fleet and pass through the east gate. The porter directs us to the great staircase on the far side of the outer courtyard, which is ringed by walls 36ft high and two-and-a-half feet thick. We pass a chapel barred by iron gates as we climb to the courtroom and pass through to the 60ft long oak-panelled dining room decorated with plaster relief ornaments on the walls and ceilings and lit with large bay windows. So far, so grand, but we have not yet reached the prison wards n on the other side of the inner courtyard, along with the workhouses equipped with treadmills for grinding flour and blocks for beating hemp. And the whipping posts.

In 1600 more than 550 vagrants were dealt with by the governors of Bridewell, compared to as few as sixty only forty years earlier (the population of London has doubled over the same period to around 250,000). Many of them have been swept up from the streets by the beadles who patrol in pairs through every ward looking for idle hands to set to work. If they refuse they can call the constable to enforce the arrest. And while some are native Londoners it seems that most originate from outside the city – from Yorkshire or East Anglia or as far west as Bristol. Most of them are young men who have either refused work or been unable to find it. Of course, the class of people known as 'vagrants' contains multitudes: fortune tellers, minstrels, bearkeepers, common players, jugglers, pedlars and tinkers operating without a licence and even common labourers who turn up their noses at what passes for the 'customary wages'. At present, we are told, there are thirty-seven vagrants, only one of which is aged over 21. The rest of the 100 or so inmates include around thirty women who are kept separately from the men and given different types of work, ranging from spinning to tennis-ball making. The women here are usually accused of being prostitutes or living with a man out of wedlock, although a few years ago a certain Mary Barton was hauled before the court for being a 'common scold' by repeatedly arguing and causing trouble with her neighbours. Other inmates include religious prisoners and foreign spies who are to be tortured into giving up their secrets. A separate part of the prison houses children over the age of twelve who are trained by 'artsmasters' in a suitable trade.

The first cell we encounter is small and narrow with no space for a bed and only a few scraps of dirty straw to rest upon. Not that you would want to lie down on the floor given that it is crawling with vermin. Indeed, the prisoner is attempting to sleep while sitting on the window ledge. But the most overwhelming feature is the suffocating smell of excrement emanating from a bucket in the corner.

In the cell next door is a man who appears little more than a skeleton. He tells us he has been fed only on bread and water and the occasional cup of ale. For the last six weeks has been ill. When we ask why he is still here, he claims it is because he has not paid his boarding fee of five groats. Prisoners are expected to pay for their stay: a penny a night to the matron and two pence a night to the porter for their beds; additional fees for the freedom of the house and the removal of leg irons; and a further two pence to the steward on release. The genuinely penniless are meant to be exempt from these charges, but there are rumours that the staff are in the habit of extracting extortionate sums as a perk of the job.

In the next room we find a group of ragged men stripped to the waist and sweating as they beat hemp upon large wooden blocks. With each repetitive THUMP of the heavy wooden mallets the tough hemp fibres are softened and split from the stalk so that they might be twisted into ropes or woven into sailcloth. It is backbreaking work and some of the inmates seem on the edge of exhaustion. But they must beat more than five pounds of hemp in order to qualify for meat for dinner. Some of these unfortunate creatures have been at it every day for eight months. We stop to ask one of the men, a surly, bull-necked fellow, what brought him to the Bridewell.

'Why if you must know I was committed hither for saying I had rather hear a blackbird whistle or a peacock scream against foul weather, than a parson talk nonsense in a church, or a fool talk Latin in a coffee house. And I'll be judged by you whether in all I said there be one word of treason to deserve a whipping post.'

Another labourer begs us with cracked lips: 'I hope you will be so generous to give us something to drink, for you don't know but we may be hard at work for you.'

We next pass on through to the treadmill, one of two such machines at Bridewell capable of setting eighteen men to work grinding corn. It is said each mill can grind 20 bushels of wheat in a day. The men at work here are in even worse condition than in the hemp-house. One prisoner is so thin and wasted, with lice swarming over him 'like ants on a molehill', that it is a wonder he can carry on going, patiently driving the mill with his feet.

These are just two of the tasks given to sturdy beggars. Others include scouring ditches or collecting rubbish from the streets, dredging the river, hauling sand or burning lime. The punishment for refusing is the whipping post. If a prisoner runs away (for there is no obstacle to them actually walking out of Bridewell) then they will be whipped through the streets at the tail of a cart.

As for the women, there are rooms to be cleaned and chamber pots to be emptied, hose to be knitted and yarn to be spun, gloves, caps and shoes to be made. In the women's quarters it smells, in one witness' words, 'as frowzy as so many goats in a Welsh gentleman's stable, or a litter of piss-tail children'. The women themselves seem more cheerful than the men despite forced to work while an overseer stalks the room with a whip. Some of the prisoners are surprisingly young and innocent-looking.

We approach one attractive woman of middling years and ask what she has done to deserve this punishment.

'If you believe me, without blushing I will tell you the truth,' she replies. 'I happened to live with an old scrivener and when my mistress was out of the way he used to tickle my lips with a pen-feather. And at last she catched us, and had me before the Justice, who committed me hither, where I have had more lashes on my poor back than ever my belly deserved since I first scattered my virginity.'

Another woman interrupts: 'Don't believe her, she's as arrant a strumpet as ever earned her living at two-pence a bout, and was committed for lying so long upon her back that her rump grew to the bottom sheet so that she could not rise again. She can show you how the watermen shoot London bridge or how the lawyers go to Westminster.'

The first woman points at the second with a smile on her face: 'What do you think this buttocking brimstone came hither for? I'll tell you – twas for picking a countryman's pocket of his pouch and hiding it in her oven. But when she came to be searched, the fool, having forgot to take up the strings, was discovered in her roguery and sent here to be lashed. Does she not deserve it, for trusting her money in a box that has neither lid nor bottom to it?'

We now return through the quadrangle to the chamber that serves as a courtroom. It is presided over by one of the Justices, a serious-looking man who is clearly distinguishable from the vagrants and prostitutes brought before him by his dress of doublet and hose. He wields a small wooden hammer, an ironic tribute to the larger version used by the inmates to beat the hemp.

First up is a prostitute sentenced to twelve lashes of the holly rods upon her bare back. This is the punishment every prisoner is given on arrival (except for children, who receive six) and it takes place in a small area adjoining the courtroom in full view of the judges. No allowance is made for the fact that she is a woman, forced to strip to the waist in front of an audience of men. The President counts each stripe upon her pale skin before knocking on his desk with the hammer to signal its end. Next up is a prisoner who has been sentenced to thirty-nine stripes. We cannot help but flinch with each blow. The victim attempts to stifle his cries but by the end he cannot help but bawl and beg for mercy: 'Knock, Sir Robert, knock.' Finally the President bangs his hammer and the man is released. It strikes us that the poor man has in fact received 468 stripes rather than thirty-nine, because the whip itself is made up of twelve knotted strings. It would have been more, he tells us, if he had not bribed the whipper with half a crown.

There are rumours too of other types of punishment delivered behind closed doors. Prisoners are clapped in manacles and suspended by their arms, or placed in the pillory, or branded, or tortured on the rack. It is said that until recently Bridewell hosted one of Skevington's

Irons (also known as Scavenger's Daughter), a device that compresses
the human body into a ball until the victim is wracked by agonising
cramps and the blood flows from their mouth, nose, fingertips and
toes.

Feeling a little queasy, we head for the exit and out into the sunlight.
This place is certainly not the palace it appears from the outside. Yet,
for all its indignities, Bridewell is an integral part of the new 'Poor
Law' established by the 1597 and 1601 Acts for the Relief of the Poor,
a major part of the attempt to solve the social problems of Elizabethan
England. This 'Poor Law' was passed after several years of bad
harvests, high corn prices, poverty and famine. The solution was relief
for the 'impotent' and work for the unemployed. Overseers of the Poor
were appointed in every parish to ensure the new regime was put into
practice. As the 1601 Act sets out:

> And they, or the greater Part of them, shall take order from Time
> to Time, by, and with the Consent of two or more such Justices of
> Peace as is aforesaid, for setting to work the Children of all such
> whose Parents shall not by the said Churchwardens and Overseers,
> or the greater Part of them. be thought able to keep and maintain
> their Children: And also for setting to work all such Persons,
> married or unmarried, having no Means to maintain them, and use
> no ordinary and daily Trade of Life to get their Living by: And also
> to raise weekly or otherwise (by Taxation of every Inhabitant,
> Parson, Vicar and other, and of every Occupier of Lands, Houses,
> Tithes impropriate, Propriations of Tithes, Coal-Mines, or saleable
> Underwoods in the said Parish, in such competent Sum and Sums
> of Money as they shall think fit) a convenient Stock of Flax, Hemp,
> Wool, Thread, Iron, and other necessary Ware and Stuff, to set the
> Poor on Work: And also competent Sums of Money for and
> towards the necessary Relief of the Lame, Impotent, Old, Blind,
> and such other among them being Poor, and not able to work, and
> also for the putting out of such Children to be apprentices, to be
> gathered out of the same Parish, according to the Ability of the
> same Parish, and to do and execute all other Things as well for the
> disposing of the said Stock, as otherwise concerning the Premisses,
> as to them shall seem convenient.'

BRIDEWELL

Bridewell became the model for dozens of other 'houses of correction' that were built in every county of England (as ordered by statute from 1609). Many of them were named after the original and the word 'bridewell' came to be used as another term for a jail. Bridewell Palace had to be rebuilt after the Great Fire of London but by the nineteenth century was functioning more as a school than a prison. It was demolished in 1864.

CHAPTER 10

Witch Hunt

*In which we attend a witch trial in Essex in 1645 and
meet the self-styled Witchfinder-General Matthew Hopkins*

A hush falls over the courtroom as the suspect is led into court before
the Justices of the Peace. It is a slow and painful process, as Elizabeth
Clarke, also known as 'Mother Bedingfield', is an 80-year-old woman
with only one leg. Her body is crooked with ill health and a life of
desperate poverty. Eventually she looks up, her toothless mouth falling
open as the justices, Sir Harbottell Grimston (who is in his seventies
himself) and Sir Thomas Bowes, begin the examination. Under
questioning, through a series of mainly yes or no answers, she reveals
how she became a witch.

About six months ago, in the autumn of 1644, she was picking up
a few sticks in a field near her home in Manningtree in Essex when a
widow named Anne West took pity on her hideous appearance. West
told her: 'There are ways and means for you to live much better than
you do now.' The widow promised to send a 'thing' like a little kitten
to her home. Two or three nights later a white Imp came to Elizabeth
Clarke as she lay in bed. The night after that it was joined by a grey
Imp. Both spoke soothingly to her, promising to find her a husband to
maintain her for the rest of her life. And after that the two creatures
came to her bed every night and suckled upon the lower parts of her
body.

Her confession at an end, Elizabeth Clarke is led away to await her
trial in Chelmsford. But is she really a witch, or just a confused, poor
old woman pushed into admitting things she does not really

understand? We seek answers to our question in the evidence of the next witness, a young man in his mid-twenties named Matthew Hopkins. He stands before us in his distinctive costume; a black, high-crowned hat, bucket-top boots and Geneva cape. His beard is trimmed short but his hair reaches almost to his shoulders. It is Hopkins who investigated the allegation of witchcraft made by one of Elizabeth Clarke's neighbours just a few days ago. A local tailor, John Rivet, believed that Clarke had bewitched his wife around Christmastime, causing her to suffer such violent fits that he feared she might die. Mr Rivet also claimed that Clarke's own mother and several other relatives had been sentenced to death for witchcraft some time ago.

Hopkins arrested the old woman and kept her under watch for several nights in an attempt to discern the truth. Yesterday, on 24 March, Elizabeth Clarke volunteered to call one of her white Imps and play with it in her lap. Shortly thereafter a series of Imps appeared in the room before vanishing. Each familiar was named in turn: Jarmara, a plump, white, stumpy-legged dog with sandy spots; a white imp named Holt; a long-legged Greyhound named Vinegar Tom; Newes, an imp resembling a Polecat; and finally a black rabbit named Sack and Sugar.

The old woman confessed she had sex with the Devil for the past six or seven years. Or, as Hopkins refers to the deed, carnal copulation. 'He would appear at her bedside three or four times a week and sleep with her in the in the form of a Gentleman with a laced band,' Hopkins explains to the court. 'He would say to her "Besse, I must lie with you", and she never once refused.'

What did the Devil want with the old woman? According to Elizabeth Clarke, Satan pestered her again and again to let him cause mischief among her neighbours in Manningtree. And so the Devil killed the hogs of Mr Edwards, and the horse of Robert Taylor. Last night Hopkins personally visited Mr Edwards to seek confirmation, only to encounter two of the witch's familiars.

'I was going from the house of Mr Edwards to my own house at about nine or ten of the Clock that night, when my greyhound suddenly gave a jump and ran off as if coursing after a hare,' he explains. 'I made haste after it and saw a white thing about the size of a Kitten dancing about the greyhound. It must have bitten my dog, for she came shrieking and crying to me with a piece of flesh torn from her shoulder. Later, as I arrived at my own yard I saw a black thing, twice the size of a cat, sitting on a strawberry bed and staring at me. I went towards it and it ran through the yard, threw open the gate and vanished.'

After Hopkins, there is confirmation from his associate John Sterne, a respectable-looking, God-fearing man in his mid-thirties, and their assistants John Banks, Frances Mills, Grace Norman, Mary Phillips, and Edward and Mary Parsley, who were all present in the room when the five imps were summoned by Elizabeth Clarke. The four women also tell the court that Clarke implicated Anne West in the death of Robert Oakes of Lawford, the child of a clothier from Dedham, and the wife of William Cole of Manningtree, who died not long ago 'from a pining and languishing disease'.

The examination then concludes. Hopkins and Stearne will continue their investigations until the next hearing.

* * *

It is now 29 July 1645. England still fights itself on the battlefield; Roundheads versus Cavaliers, Parliamentarians versus Royalists, brother versus brother. The people are described as 'wasted, exhausted, tired out, ready to give up the ghost, hardly anything left to cover their nakedness or their children bread to eat'. Cities are besieged, raised and ransacked. Families are losing their homes and livelihoods and even the richest are at risk of becoming poor. Lady Ann Fanshawe, who until the age of 17 enjoyed a comfortable existence supported by her father Sir John Harrison, was forced to flee to a dingy room in Oxford. 'From as good houses as any gentleman of England had, we came to a baker's house in an obscure street,' she explains, 'and from rooms well-furnished to lie in a very bad bed in a garret, to one dish of meat and that not the best ordered; no money, for we were as poor as Job, nor clothes more than a man or two brought in their cloak bags. We had the perpetual discourse of losing and gaining of towns and

74

men; at the windows the sad spectacle of war, sometimes plague, sometimes sicknesses of other kind, by reason of so many people being packed together as I believe there never was before of that quality; always want, yet I must needs say that most bore it with a martyr-like cheerfulness.'

Others of less noble birth suffered the confiscation of their property by rampaging soldiers. Thomas Tasker, who describes himself as 'a poor and aged' labourer of Epwell in Oxfordshire, was woken in the middle of the night in December 1644 by a group of Roundhead soldiers under the command of Major George Purefoy. They took him prisoner and ransacked his house of everything of value, including sheets, brass kettles, pewter dishes, pans, cutlery, clothes, boots, candles, and a basket of eggs. To add insult to robbery, the Major bombarded him with 'harsh speeches' and refused to let him have a single word in reply before finally releasing him five days later. Of course, the homeless and unemployed could always find a job as a soldier, with a wage similar to that of a farm labourer.

The worst hit areas are in the North and Midlands, while London and the south-east has escaped relatively unscathed. But there are signs the conflict is drawing to a close after Charles' armies were defeated at Naseby and Langport. Just a few days ago Bridgewater in Somerset fell to the New Model Army of Thomas Fairfax and Oliver Cromwell.

Meanwhile Essex, which has seen little military action during the Civil War, concerns itself with the fate of a suspected witches' coven centred on Manningtree, a town of narrow, winding streets situated on an estuary with pleasant views of green fields, trees, ponds and mudflats stretching out to the sea.

Elizabeth Clarke, that confused and harmless-looking old woman, has been sentenced to death for witchcraft. She is one of more than a dozen to be hanged today in Chelmsford thanks to the evidence gathered by Hopkins and Stearne. Their star witness at the trial was Rebecca West, the 15-year-old daughter of 'the old Beldam' Anne West. Her story, recounted at the bar before Robert, Earl of Warwick and Judge Coniers, unfurled as follows:

Last Shrovetide her mother Anne took her aside after work and made her promise never to say a word about what she was to witness that evening. The sun was setting as she was led to a house across the fields and introduced to four elderly women, Elizabeth Clarke, Elizabeth Gooding, Anne Leech and Helen Clark. This was to be her initiation ceremony, led by the two senior witches of the group, Clarke and Gooding (known to her as Mother Benefield and Mother Goodwin). A book was produced and a prayer read. Then the Imps appeared. Six of them took the form of week-old kittens. Mother Benefield put them in her lap and kissed them in turn, telling Rebecca: 'These are all my children by as handsome a man as any in England.' Next the witches commanded their familiars to kill a man's Horse, a cow, and a child. And then Mother Benefield warned Rebecca that if she told anyone what happened that night then she would suffer 'more tortures and pains on earth than the pains of Hell'. To ensure her loyalty, she was forced to take the Oath, to deny God and the Saviour Jesus Christ and instead worship only Satan. And once she had renounced her Christian beliefs, the Devil appeared in the shape of a little black dog, leapt into her lap and kissed her three times with a cold mouth. The final part of this initiation ceremony took place later that night when the Devil appeared again in the form of a dashing young man. He took her by the hand and led her around the room while she recited an oath: 'I Rebecca take thee to be my husband and do promise to be an obedient wife till death, faithfully to perform and observe all thy commands.'

Her evidence confirmed the statement she gave Matthew Hopkins back in March. But why would she testify against her own mother? Was she told her life would be spared in exchange for implicating the four older women? Or was she threatened? Rumours are spreading that the Witchfinders have employed questionable methods to secure confessions. It is claimed that 80-year-old Elizabeth Clarke was left sitting on a stool without rest for hours upon end. Denied sleep and the chance to stretch tired, cramping limbs, it is perhaps no surprise that the old woman confessed to witchcraft.

Although physical torture is now illegal (except in some approved circumstances) *mental* hardship is not forbidden. The former King

James I, who wrote books on the subject of witchcraft, was in favour of using a little forceful persuasion to ensure a witch was convicted and condemned to death. It is his law, passed in 1604, that the Witchfinders are seeking to enforce:

> If any person shall use practise or exercise any invocation or conjuration of any evil and wicked spirit or shall consult, covenant with, entertain, employ, feed or reward any evil or wicked spirit, to or for any intent and purpose, or take up any dead man, woman or child out of their graves, or the skin, bone or any part of the dead person to be used in any manner of witchcraft, sorcery or enchantment, whereby any person shall be killed, destroyed, wasted, consumed, pined or lamed in his or her body, that then every such offender, their aiders, abettors and counsellors shall suffer the pains of death.

In addition to seeking confessions, the Witchfinders are using a series of tests. The ancient rite of 'swimming' involves tying a suspect's thumbs to their toes and casting them into the water. If she floats, it is a sure sign of guilt. Witches also have the Devil's marks or 'witches teats' which are suckled on by their familiars. Further confirmation can be provided by the appearance of Imps, such as rats or even beetles.

But surely even Witchfinders float in water? And who can distinguish between a witches teat and a wart, or a clitoris, or a haemorrhoid? And why are so many of the convicted witches poor, elderly women living alone? One witness to the trial at Chelmsford (Arthur Wilson, the Earl of Warwick's steward), tells us that he 'could see nothing in the evidence which did persuade me to think them other than poor, melancholy, envious, mischievous, ill disposed, ill-dieted, atra-bilious constitutions, whose fancies worked on gross fumes and vapours . . . and if there be an opinion in the people that such a body is a witch, their own fears resulting from such dreadful apprehension, do make every shadow an apparition, and every rat or cat an imp or spirit, which make so many tales and stories in the world, which have no shadow of truth.'

Seeking answers, we set off in search of Hopkins and Stearne, who have left Essex and headed to their home county of Suffolk to investigate other witches named in their so-called 'Devil's List'.

* * *

We finally catch up with Hopkins in Manningtree in the early summer of 1647. The King has been defeated and is now a prisoner of Parliament in Northamptonshire. As to what will come next, it is hard to tell. As for Hopkins, he is suffering from consumption, an illness which may have already claimed his father some thirteen years ago. For the past two years he has travelled through Essex, Suffolk, Norfolk, Huntingdonshire, and Cambridgeshire. In that time they have secured the conviction of more than 200 witches, the vast majority of them women. But while many support their activities (and pay them handsomely for it), the objections grow stronger. The Reverend John Gaule, has openly attacked Hopkins, the self-proclaimed Witchfinder General, in his church sermons. He has even published his criticisms in a pamphlet: 'Every old woman with a wrinkled face, a furred brow, a hairy lip, a gobber tooth, a squint eye, a squeaking voice or a scolding tongue, having a rugged coat on her back, a skull cap on her head, a spindle in her hand and a dog or cat by her side is not only suspected but pronounced for a witch. Hopkins' signs discover no other witch but the user of them.'

What does Hopkins say of these claims? How does he distinguish a witch from a confused old woman?

'It comes from experience,' he replies, 'which though it be meanly esteemed of, yet the surest and safest way to judge by.'

Hopkins explains how he discovered the Manningtree witches. 'Every six weeks on a Friday night they had their meeting close by my house and offered their solemn sacrifices to the Devil. I heard one of speaking to her Imps one night. She was apprehended and searched and found to have three teats about her, which honest women have not.'

He confirms the suspected witch – Elizabeth Clarke – was

prevented from sleeping for two or three nights, but adds that he was under command of the Justice of the Peace. It was only by doing so that the Witch was caught out summoning her Imps by name: Holt, Jarmara, Vinegar Tom, Sack and Sugar and Newes. More importantly, she named other witches in the county. 'In our Hundred in Essex,' he boasts, 'twenty-nine were condemned at once.' Four of them tried to take revenge by sending a bear to kill him in his garden.

We ask how he can condemn a person simply for having a teat on their body, which may have natural causes such as piles or childbirth. Hopkins says there are three reasons why the marks are 'not merely natural'. Firstly: 'I judge by the unusualnes of the place where I findeth the teats in or on their bodies. If a witch plead the marks found are haemorrhoids, then if I find them on the bottom of the back-bone, shall I assent?' Secondly they are insensitive to pain: 'They feel neither pin, needle, or awl thrust through them.' Thirdly, these marks often mutate into several forms. 'If a Witch hears a month or two before that the Witchfinder is coming, they will put out their Imps to others to suckle them, even to their own young and tender children.' In these cases Hopkins keeps the suspect under watch for 24 hours to make sure none of her Imps are allowed to suckle. 'The next day after her teats will have extended out to their former filling length, full of corruption ready to burst.'

So what about the allegations he tortured the suspected witches by preventing them from sleeping for three nights and forcing them to walk until their feet blistered?

Hopkins claims that these practices were authorised the Magistrates in Essex and Suffolk. He says: 'Seldom did any Witch ever complain in the time of their keeping for want of rest, it was only after they had beat their heads together in Gaol.' They stopped using this tactic a year and a half ago, he insists. 'Since then only their own stubborn wills did not let them sleep, though it was offered to them.'

What of the swimming test?

Hopkins smiles: 'It is not denied that those with paps floated, while others that had none were tried with them and sunk.' The reason, as stated in King James' *Demonology*, is that the witch is rejected by the water because she has denied her baptism by making her pact with the Devil. 'But it was never used against any of them as evidence at their trials,' he adds.

We now ask Hopkins about the supposed confessions. Did he obtain them by frightening the poor old women? Or put words into their mouths when they were confused by lack of sleep?

Hopkins says: 'When a Witch is first found with teats, then removed from her house, which is only to keep her old associates from her, and so by good counsel brought into a sad condition, by understanding of the horribleness of her sin, and the judgements threatened against her; and knowing the Devils malice and subtle circumventions, is brought to remorse and sorrow for complying with Satan so long, and disobeying Gods sacred Commands, doth then desire to unfold her mind with much bitterness, and of her own accord declare what was the occasion of the Devils appearing to her, what speech they had, what likeness he was in, what voice be had, what familiars he sent her, what number of spirits, what names they had, what shape they were in, what employment she set them about to several persons in several places, all which mischief being proved to be done, is testimony enough against her.'

Hopkins insists he does not rely on any confession gained through torture, or threat of violence, or by flattery. He also rejects any confession that involves an impossibility such as 'flying in the air, riding on a broom, and so on.'

Hopkins denies he was motivated by money, despite evidence he could have earned more than £1,000 over the past two years. He says he demanded only 20 shillings a town to cover his travel, his bed and board, wages for his associates and the maintenance of three horses. Hopkins adds: 'I never went to any town or place unless they sent for me, and they were happy to do so.'

Matthew Hopkins appears to have died of consumption in August 1647. The death sentence for witchcraft (under the Witchcraft Acts of 1562 and 1604) ended in 1735. From then on anybody claiming to be a witch or to have magical powers faced a maximum prison sentence of twelve months. The last person to be convicted of witchcraft was the 72-year-old medium Jane Yorke in 1944. She was fined £5.

The Civil War also saw the rise of the Levellers Movement, which petitioned Parliament for regular elections, free trade, the abolition of tithes, religious toleration, 'some effectual course to keep people from begging and beggary' and the reversal of recent enclosures of common lands. It also called for the vote to be given to all men 21 or over except servants or paupers receiving alms. The Levellers were crushed by Oliver Cromwell in 1649 and electoral rights were not reformed until 1832. Following the execution of King Charles I, Cromwell ruled as Lord Protector until his death in 1658. Two years later the monarchy was restored under Charles II.

CHAPTER 11

At the Fair

In which we experience the sights and sounds of
Bartholomew's Fair in London in the late seventeenth century

'Buy a mousetrap, a mousetrap, or a tormentor for a flea?'
'Ballads! Ballads! Fine new ballads!'
'Buy some gingerbread?'
'What do you lack, ladies and gentlemen?'
'Buy any pears, pears, fine, very fine pears!'
The cries of the fair bombard us from all sides, drawing us ever deeper into the mass of booths laden with everything you might possibly want, and more besides. It is as if all of London is crammed into the space between St Bartholomew's hospital for the poor and the cattle market at Smithfield just outside the city walls.

Here is the toymaker's stall, decked out in rattles, drums, hobby horses and dolls, the last known as 'Bartholomew Babies'. He repeats his call: 'What do you lack? What is't you buy? Halberts, horses, babies o' the best, fiddles of the finest! Maid, see a fine hobby-horse for your young master. What do you buy, mistress? A fine hobby-horse, to make your son a tilter? A drum, to make him a soldier? A fiddle, to make him a reveller? What is't you lack? Little dogs for your daughters, or babies, male or female?'

Next is Ursula the Pig Woman, who cooks the finest pork in the city. A sign above her booth shows a pig's head speaking the words: 'Here be the best pigs and she does roast them as well as she ever did'. Ursula spots the salivating gaze of a young girl and calls out to her: 'A delicate show-pig, little mistress, with sweet sauce and crackling.

You shalt have the clean side of the table-cloth, and the glass washed.'
And now appealing to another group: 'Gentlewomen, the weather's
hot; whither walk you? Have a care of your fine velvet caps; the fair
is dusty. Take a sweet, delicate booth with boughs, here in the way,
and cool yourselves in the shade, you and your friends. The best pig
and bottle-ale in the fair, sir.'

We move on past a wrestler slumped on the ground, tired from
competing in the annual bout before the Lord Mayor. That, and the
buckets of ale he has downed since.

The cries continue, relentless, as we push through the crowds.

'Buy any gingerbread, gilt gingerbread! Will your worship buy any
gingerbread? Very good bread, comfortable bread!'

'Buy any ballads? New ballads! Hey!'

'Have you any corns on your feet and toes?'

'What do you lack, gentlemen? Fine purses, pouches, pin-cases,
pipes? A pair o' smiths, to wake you in the morning, or a fine whistling
bird?'

The ballad seller now starts to sing: 'My masters and friends and
good people draw near, and look to your purses for that I do say, and
though little money in them you do bear, it costs more to get than to
lose in a day. You oft have been told, both the young and the old, and
bidden beware of the cut-purse so bold.'

The pickpockets are another traditional feature of Bartholomew's
Fair. No doubt they were here when it started more than 500 years ago.
It was 1123 when Henry I's former jester, Rahere, founded the Priory
of St Bartholomew on a muddy patch of land next to the King's
Market. One of the first visitors was a notorious poor man who had
lost the use of his legs and dragged his body around London for many
years. Yet, as soon as he had offered prayers at the altar his crooked
limbs were healed. Many others flocked to the church in the hope of
similar miracles.

The fair grew out of the traditional gathering of worshippers and
pilgrims on the feast day of St Bartholomew on 24 August. Over time
it lost its religious overtones and became more famous as a cloth fair
before turning into a haunt of pleasure-seekers. The Lord Mayor of

London, dressed in his scarlet gown and golden chain, opens proceedings by reading a proclamation. This is followed by a wrestling competition and a rabbit-chase (in which a sack of live rabbits is set free to be pursued through the crowds by determined young boys). As well as booths and stalls there are puppet shows, freakshows, sideshows, plays and exhibitions. You will find prize-fighters and acrobats competing for your money with a camel and a child with three legs and sixteen toes. It is a far cry from the gruesome public executions held here before the gallows were moved to Tyburn in the reign of Queen Elizabeth. The Scottish rebel William Wallace was hanged, disembowelled, beheaded and dismembered on this very spot on 23 August 1305, the eve of the feast of St Bartholomew.

Although the fair did not take place in the plague years of 1625, 1630, 1665 and 1666, it was not touched by the fire which swept through London and destroyed the Guildhall and St Paul's Cathedral as well as countless ramshackle wooden houses. Thousands fled their burning homes to camp out in the open fields of Islington and Highgate or move to the countryside or even abroad. London is now being rebuilt in stone. Meanwhile the people seek to distract themselves from their worries by taking in the fun of the fair. Its renown attracts visitors of all sorts and conditions; high and low, rich and poor, from the city or the countryside, regardless of gender or religious persuasion. Perhaps Catherine, the Queen of England herself, is here today disguised as an Essex lass in a red petticoat buying a pair of yellow stockings for her lover. Or the magistrate Samuel Pepys, hoping to catch the eye of a buxom lady or three.

One of the most popular shows is put on by the company of ropedancers. The performers risk their limbs walking, prancing and tumbling across the rope, apparently unfazed by its height above the pavement. We stop to watch as an Italian with a duck on his head dances along one perilously sloping cord while pushing a wheelbarrow containing two children and a dog. The crowd shows its appreciation with deafening shouts, gales of laughter and hearty applause.

Now we move on to the gates of the hospital which was seized by Henry VIII before being handed over to the city in 1547. To enter them you have to be poor as well as sick. There you will be cared for by fifteen nursing sisters in blue cloth dresses and fed a diet of 12 ounces of bread, eight ounces of beef or mutton or butter and cheese, one pint of meat broth or porridge and three pints of hospital beer. One wonders whether the patients are let out at fair time – surely they must be able to hear this great din of human pleasure outside?

Talking of pleasure, we should not forget the 'catalogue of jilts, cracks, prostitutes, night walkers, whores, she-friends, kind women and others of the Linen-lifting tribe' who can be seen at fair time between 8pm and 11pm. There is Mrs Mary H, who is described as 'a tall, graceful, comely woman, indebted for two thirds of her beauty to washes and the patch-box' and may grant you her favours in return for a present of silver furniture costing £20. On the other end of the scale is Dorothy R, 'a tall comely woman, a little red faced by drinking too much usqebagh', who costs just 1s 4d.

Near the gate there is an advertisement for an 'Indian King' – a dark-skinned man in Indian dress who can be viewed for two pence. Past him, next door to the Golden Hart sign you can see a woman with three breasts, all of which can express milk, it is claimed. Another booth demands sixpence (with a shilling for the best seats) to see 'A Prodigious Monster being a man with one head and two distinct bodies, both masculine'. Then finally, a 'changeling child, aged nine years and more not exceeding a foot and a half high'.

Our tour complete, we plunge back into the crowds once more.

'Here, mister, see the Tall Dutchwoman!'

'Buy a pretty doll.'

'See The Tiger!'

'What do you lack, what do you buy?'

Bartholomew's Fair was shortened from two weeks to four days in 1691 and during the eighteenth century gradually grew less popular until its abolition was discussed in 1798. The exhibitions were banned in 1840 and the Lord Mayor read the last proclamation in 1850. It took place for the final time in 1855.

CHAPTER 12

Bedlam

*In which we speak to the patients of the Bethlehem Hospital,
commonly known as Bedlam, in London in the
early eighteenth century*

Two naked, shaven-headed statues greet us at the entrance to England's
first public asylum. The first reclines gloomily on a plinth in only a
loincloth. The second, his wrists chained together, fixes us with a
manic stare. They represent the two forms of mental illness to be found
here, Melancholy and Raving Madness.

Bedlam, like Bridewell Prison, is often mistaken for a royal palace.
Finished in 1676, it was modelled on Louis XIV's 'Chateaux de
Tuilleries' and boasts long, wide galleries, stone balustrades, and a
central turret adorned with a clock, a gilt ball and a weathervane. It is
in fact home to some of the most vulnerable of society, the 'lunatics'
and 'unfortunate wretches' who have no relatives to look after them
or money to pay for their care. Up to 120 patients can be held here at
one time with the men in the east wing and the women in the west.
The most dangerous are kept chained up on the second floor but the
most harmless are allowed to wander the galleries under supervision.

We pass through an iron gate into the building and are immediately
bombarded with a cacophony of noise; rattling chains, banging doors,
stamping feet, shouting, moaning, weeping and singing. The din grows
louder as we pass into the east gallery, 193 yards long with thirty-eight 12ft
long cells lining either side. Each cell door has a window to allow the public
to observe the patient in their natural habitat. Visiting Bedlam is a popular
pastime, particularly on holidays, and there are several other people here
satisfying their curiosity (or, it seems, to have fun at the patients' expense).

BEDLAM

The first man we see, who wanders freely up and down the gallery, grabs us by the arm as we walk past. When we ask him what brought him to Bedlam, he replies: 'I am under confinement for the noble sins of drinking and whoring, and if thou hast not a care it will bring thee into the same condition.' The noble drunkard then points out another man nearby, who is said to be a Cambridge scholar and a musician. 'He is a fiddling fellow, who had so many crotchets in his head that he cracked his brains.'

Moving on we see another fellow peeping through the hole in his door while chewing happily on bread and cheese.

'Bread is good with cheese, and cheese is good with bread and bread and cheese is good together,' he says. We nod in agreement. Suddenly he sneezes violently, projecting mangled bread and cheese in every direction. We move back, but he begs us to return: 'Masters, masters,' he cries. Then, just as we near his door again he flings a bowlful of stinking urine in our faces.

He laughs. 'I never give victuals, but I give drink, and you're welcome gentleman.'

Gingerly approaching a room further down the corridor we detect the distinctive odour of ammonia, or 'chamber-lye'. Inside a man is stamping his feet on the ground as if working a treadmill. We ask what he is doing.

'I am trampling down conscience under my feet, lest he should rise up and fly in my face. Have a care he does not fright thee, for he looks like the devil and is as fierce as a lion, but that I keep him muzzled. Therefore get thee gone, or I will set him upon thee.' He then claps his hands and shouts 'Hallooo'.

The Hallooos still ring in our ears as we look in through the next window to spy on a ragged man dressed in a faded red army uniform with a broken broomstick thrust through a hole in his coat as if it were a sword. He appears to be barking orders to his troops but the only other living beings present in his cell are flies and vermin, none of which are paying any attention to his commands.

Our tour now takes us to the women's wing. Iron grills separate it from the male side to prevent coupling between patients and each cell has a lock that can only be opened by the matron to stop the male orderlies, or 'basketmen', getting up to mischief. As we enter the gallery we hear a woman shouting, with her back to the wall: 'Hark, hark, run, you rogue, your master's come back to shop. Fie, for shame, out upon't! A husband for a woman, a husband or the devil! Hang you, rot you, sink you confound you!'

In another room a young woman sits upon a straw bed with her eyes shut, gasping for breath with her tongue protruding out of her mouth.

Next door to her a woman reveals that she ended up in Bedlam because of 'love'. She tells us: 'I was a Mantua maker and I lived in Covent Garden. But being ignorant of the ways of the town I began an intrigue with a young man. Because I had a jealous old aunt living with me I was obliged to send my lover a suit of clothes and in this disguise he was admitted into my bedchamber. Yet while we endeavoured to play in and in, the devil a ladle he put in my kettle.'

Further down a group of young women crowd around the cell of 'Bess of Bedlam'. One of them asks how old Bess is, to which she replies: 'I am old enough to have hair where you have none.'

Most of the patients here are poor men and women who have been sent here by their local magistrate or parish authorities because of their disturbing behaviour. Bedlam has been looking after paupers since 1247 when the Priory of St Mary of Bethlehem was founded. Bethlehem Hospital quickly became known as 'Bethlem'. At that time it was based in a much smaller, one-storey building in Bishopsgate in central London. By the early fifteenth century it was a dedicated mental hospital with six 'lunatic' patients, six sets of chains, four manacles and two stocks. After the dissolution of the monasteries it was placed first under the control of the Corporation of London and then the governors of Bridewell. As its notoriety grew it became known as 'Bedlam'. In Shakespeare's time a type of vagrant was named after it: the Tom O'Bedlam was a devious rogue who pretended to be mad to earn sympathy (and more importantly food, drink and money).

There were also rumours of mismanagement, squalid conditions, beatings and sexual scandal. In 1632 a Royal Commission discovered the Keeper Helkiah Crooke was cooking the books, stealing funds and even selling items donated for the upkeep of pauper patients. An inspection uncovered decaying walls, an empty kitchen and rampant starvation among the poorer patients who could not afford to buy their own food.

By the 1660s more and more people were being sent to asylums instead of being cared for at home by their families. Bedlam, which had room for only fifty-nine patients, was flooded with applications and was clearly in need of replacement. The new hospital that we stand in now was built in 1676 on open ground just north of the City in Moorfields, at a cost of £17,000.

The patients are now treated by a visiting physician who is paid around a guinea a visit. Dr Edward Tyson, who was the 'mad doctor' at Bedlam from 1684 until his death in 1708, was known for his kindness to the mentally ill. Dr Tyson's favoured treatment for mental illness was a bath in freezing water, which he believed 'preserves the spirits from evaporation, strengthens all the nervous parts, stops the evacuation of humours and helps the circulation'. Other doctors prefer more drastic treatments such as bloodletting, forced vomiting and confinement in a dark room for six weeks.

Another spectator at Bedlam tells us that the asylum is also a popular courting spot for couples. 'Tis a new Whetstone's Park, where a sportsman may meet with game for his purpose. Thought they came in single, they went out in pairs.' He adds with a smile: 'Tis an almshouse for madmen, a showing room for whores, a sure market for lechers and a dry walk for loiterers.'

It is time to leave. We hand the porter a penny as we walk out of the gates and bid Bedlam goodbye.

England's second public asylum was built in Norwich in 1713. It was followed by Manchester in 1752, Newcastle in 1765 and Liverpool in 1797. By 1845 every county in England was required to have a lunatic asylum. Bedlam continued to admit visitors until 1770. It was rebuilt at St George's Fields in Southwark in 1815 and in 1930 moved to Bromley. It is now known as Bethlem Royal Hospital.

CHAPTER 13

The Common Side

In which we find ourselves cast into the Marshalsea,
one of the three main debtor's prisons in London, in 1729

There are two sides to Marshalsea Debtors' Prison. And though they are separated only by a few old wooden boards, they are as different as Heaven and Hell.

The Master's Side is reserved for prisoners who can borrow enough money from friends and relatives to pay for a relatively comfortable double room (2s 6d a week), clean sheets and laundry, a haircut at the in-house barber, cooked meals from Tiddy-Doll's Chop House or Mother Bradshaw's Coffee Room (ham and salad, or veal knuckle, bacon and cauliflowers, or fried whiting), and down bottles of wine while watching dances in the Great Hall in the company of temporarily impoverished writers, musicians, businessmen, pimps, bauds, gamblers and even the Governor himself.

The Common Side houses destitute paupers who cannot even afford to pay off a debt of one shilling. Their punishment is to be crowded into damp single-sex dormitories holding up to forty at a time, half of them lying on a filthy floor swarming with vermin and half suspended above them on hammocks. The only entertainment is provided by a stinking pisspot in the centre of the room and the daily battle with starvation.

It is our misfortune to be allocated a dormitory about 14ft long and 11ft wide known as Duke's Ward (it is a cruel joke that all the wards on the Common Side are given noble titles including Queen and Duchess for the women and King and Prince for the men). There are thirty-two other prisoners crammed into here already. The 'constable', a senior prisoner chosen by a majority vote, demands we pay our 'garnish money' of four shillings and sixpence in addition to the 4 pence admission fee and the 15 pence steward's fee. As we do not have it (we surely would have paid for a bed on the Master's Side if we did), our clothes are stripped from our backs. We are told we will get them back when we pay up.

Naked apart from the odd rag to cover our modesty, we slump despondently on to a dirty patch of straw on one side of the room. The wards are locked at 9pm but sleep is elusive. At ten the prisoners shout greetings and abuse from one ward to another while the sick, starving and wounded sigh and groan. Meanwhile our senses are attacked by crawling insects, noxious smells and a constant gnawing hunger.

The wards are opened again at dawn (8am in winter and 5am in summer). Inmates are free to wander around the 'Castle' and breathe some marginally cleaner air in the yard, known to them as the 'Park'. This too is split into two sides. In the Common Side of the Park our fellow prisoners urinate in the cups meant to be used to drink from the water pump, or stare eagerly at anyone who has managed to save a bit of bread to eat.

Food is the biggest problem on the Common Side. Prisoners are supposed to receive a share of the charitable donations given to the Marshalsea but it is well known that most of them are stolen by the Governor, a former butcher named William Acton. He held the post of Master Turnkey before paying £400 a year rent to run the prison. It is a profitable enterprise – Acton makes more than £500 a year from the Master's Side alone in addition to rents from the prison pub, coffee room and chophouse. But that does not stop Acton extracting as much as possible from his poorest inmates. It is reckoned that if he had distributed the charity money to the prisoners (estimated to be at least £115 a year), then each of them would have received 2lbs of bread a week. Acton has also been confiscating the money and victuals given to prisoners begging 'at the grate' by passing merchants, shopkeepers and tradesmen. All they are left with is a share of the weekly donation of 30lbs of beef from the judge and officers of the Marshalsea. This amounts to perhaps an ounce and a half of meat and a quarter of a halfpenny loaf for the residents of the sick ward, with the rest divided among wards. But there are so many people here (319 at the last count, including sixty-eight women) that they are lucky to receive their share once a week.

It is reckoned that between eight and ten prisoners die every day.

Some are so desperate for food that the only alternative is to attempt an escape. One man who tried was a poor carpenter named Thomas Bliss. In October 1726 he attempted to climb out using a rope. The rope broke and he fell to the ground, damaging his ankle. Acton's men seized Bliss, stamped on his belly, beat him with a truncheon made from a dried bull's penis and clapped the irons on his legs. He was then tortured into confessing which member of staff gave him the rope. Thumbscrews were used on both hands and an iron skull cap was placed on his head and tightened until blood flowed from his ears and nose. Bliss begged for mercy. Acton replied: 'Damn ye, tell me who brought ye the rope!' He was then cast into a dark, damp cell known as the Strong Room and secured to an iron ring in the middle of the floor by large iron fetters attached to his legs. When his wife Anne came to visit and peered through a small hole in the door she saw his whole body was black with bruises and his stomach was so swollen that his clothes had to be cut off. His mouth was so sore that he could only eat food once it had been chewed by a fellow inmate. By the time he was let out a few days later, Bliss was effectively lame. He was eventually released from prison without paying his debt but enjoyed only a few months of freedom before dying in March 1727.

Even more horrific is the case of Captain James Thompson, who was locked in the Strong Room overnight simply because he had diabetes. When a fellow inmate complained that Thompson was likely to die, Acton replied: 'What is that to you, ye old son of a bitch, let him die and be damn'd.' When the door was unlocked the next morning, Thompson was indeed dead. His eye, his cheek and part of his ear had been eaten by rats.

We try not to imagine our own fate. Most likely we will slowly starve until we are carried to the sick ward, a miserable room where prisoners are stacked in three levels: the first row on the floor, the second on trestles and the third in hammocks suspended from the ceiling. Some of them are so weak and malnourished that if you give them solid food they die attempting to digest it.

It is hard to imagine a more pathetic death.

Conditions in the Marshalsea improved following an inspection by a committee of MPs in 1729. The enquiry led to the prosecution of William Acton for the murder of four prisoners including Thomas Bliss and James Thompson. He was acquitted of all charges at the Kingston Assizes after testifying (supported by his servants) that the Strong Room was the best room in the prison. Later that year he was removed from his post and became the landlord of the Greyhound Pub across the road. The Marshalsea survived the Gordon Riots (thirty rioters were killed in an attempt to destroy it) and in 1824 Charles Dickens' father was sent there because he owed money to a baker. Imprisonment for debt was only abolished in 1869.

CHAPTER 14

Gin

*In which we experience the delights of the 'Gin Craze'
of Georgian London in c. 1740*

In an unremarkable street in the London parish of St Luke's a crowd of people waits impatiently to receive its fix. They appear to be queuing up behind a sign nailed to the window of a house. The sign is in the shape of a cat. Curious, we join the excited throng pressing into Blue Anchor Alley. Up ahead we notice men, women and even a few children sipping and gulping from cups, smacking their lips and sighing in pleasure. A few rejoin the noisy queue to be served. Others lean sleepy-eyed against walls and fences, or slump in the road. One appears to be vomiting happily into the gutter. There is only one explanation: Gin.

Eventually we near the sign. The man in front of us posts a few coins through a slot in the cat's mouth and says the magic words: 'Puss, give me two pennyworth of Gin.' A voice bids the man to prepare to receive it from the lead pipe under the cat's paw. The man, who has not brought his own cup or seen fit to borrow one, places his mouth directly under the funnel. A moment later the pipe gurgles and liquid pours down his throat. Two pennies will get you perhaps a quarter of Gin. Not a lot, but enough to light a fire in your throat and belly and put a new complexion on things.

It is now our turn. We approach the sign and go through the same ritual to receive our own two-pennyworth. It tastes strongly of cheap spirits flavoured with fruit and sugar, almost like punch. But why is it so popular? For centuries the poor have been drinking beer and ale.

Now they drink Gin. And lots of it. It is reckoned that seven million gallons of Gin are consumed in England every year (compared to three million gallons of beer). That equals two gallons for every adult. And it seems that women like Gin just as much as men. Perhaps even more. It is as if Gin is the latest fashion which no inhabitant of London can ignore.

They say this craze began fifty years ago when William III decided to tax Gin and other distilled spirits to fund his wars against France. You might have thought that higher taxes would mean lower demand, but Gin continued to gain in popularity. Soon the taxes on spirits were providing the Crown with a tenth of its annual income. Because of this Parliament was unwilling to regulate the sale of Gin and outlets sprang up all over the city. Men and women sold it in the street as a sideline business to add to their earnings from their usual trades. This increase in competition (and the low price of grain used to make spirits) led to cheaper Gin. What was previously the preserve of high society became available to all. Even a lowly maid could afford a thousand cups of Gin with her annual wage.

The result is a craze for Gin that has shocked 'respectable' citizens who preferred to get drunk indoors and among their own kind. 'Whoever shall pass among the streets will find wretches stretched upon the pavement, insensible and motionless,' says Lord Lonsdale, 'and others more dangerous who have drank too much to fear punishment, but not enough to hinder them from provoking it, who think themselves in the elevation of drunkenness entitled to treat all those with contempt whom their dress distinguishes from them.' Gin is blamed for increases in crime, the number of poor people in the streets and the idleness and disorder of the population in general. 'Gin shops are undoubtedly the nurseries of all manner of vice and wickedness,' says the magistrate Henry Fielding.

It is the women drinkers that worry them most, the women who bear the children destined to work in the factories and fight for the glory of Great Britain. What kind of children will these women bring forth if they are drunk all day? What about Judith Defour, a poor silk spinner (a 'throwster') who, in 1734, strangled her two-year-old daughter, left her body in a field and sold her clothing to buy Gin? Or the women who drank so much Gin that they suddenly burst into flames?

Parliament decided to crack down on the Gin Craze by passing the Gin Act of 1736, banning the sale of Gin without a licence (costing a hefty £50) and setting the tax at 20 shillings per gallon. A £5 reward was offered to informers and anyone caught selling the spirit illegally would have to pay £10 to the informer or be sent to prison for two months.

The Gin Act failed, despite sending over 4,000 people – many of them women – to Bridewell Prison and gathering £30,000 in fines. In fact it was so unsuccessful that more Gin was drunk in England than ever before. People just found a way to get around the rules, whether by diluting the taxed Gin until it could be sold at a reasonable price or devising cunning methods to sell Gin on the sly. This explains the enterprise in Blue Anchor Alley, off Bunhill Row near the Artillery Ground. The Gin shop at the sign of the cat was set up by an Irish adventurer named Dudley Bradstreet, who bought £13 worth of Gin and rented a house anonymously through an acquaintance to serve as his shop. Business was slow at first but as word spread throughout the neighbourhood his daily takings increased from six shillings to £4. By the end of the month he had made £22. His successful scheme is now being imitated across the city with what are being called 'Puss and Mew' shops. Hand over your money with the codeword 'Puss' and the cat will supply you with Gin with a friendly 'Mew'.

Other Gin shops are operated from single rented rooms occupied by the families of labourers, shoemakers, chandlers, greengrocers, fruiterers, cooks and watermen. You will find one example at the home of the cobblers Daniel Clay, his wife Elizabeth and their two-year-old daughter Eleanor in Wapping, east London. They sell Gin to other shoemakers in the area but are not averse to sampling it themselves. Even young Eleanor joins in, it seems, as she is often seen tumbling about the floor in drunken befuddlement.

And you will always find Gin sellers wherever the 'The Mob' gathers in search of entertainment. 'No modern mob can long subsist without their darling cordial, the grand preservative of sloth, Geneva', says Edward Withers. 'The traders, who vend it among them on these occasions, are commonly the very rubbish of the creation, the worst of both sexes, but most of them weather beaten fellows that have misspent their youth.'

Outside Newgate Prison we find one such Mob waiting for the condemned men to be taken to Tyburn. As the criminals are led out the gate the crowd surges forward with them, pushing and shoving, kicking and tripping each other up while the constables shepherd them with sticks designed to crack heads. We notice an old man in a putrefied wig, hemmed into corner offering a dram of Gin to passers-by. Another seller dressed in rags shouts himself hoarse as he moves along the edges of the crowd holding a basketful of bottles. A third attempts to do business in the middle of the torrent of people. And over on the side of the street a young woman sells Gin while her old, decrepit mother slumps drunkenly against a shopfront. Eventually the din lessens as the crowd moves off towards the scene of execution.

As we turn to leave, a few rogues raise a drunken cheer: 'No Gin, no King.'

The 'Gin Craze' started to fade away during the 1740s and sales of the spirit were already decreasing when the 1751 Gin Act was passed. This law increased taxes, banned small-scale distillers and favoured the sale of Gin by respectable retailers. Prices increased and Gin regained its reputation as a middle-class drink.

CHAPTER 15

Foundlings

*In which we visit the Foundling Hospital in London
on the day in 1756 it receives 117 children into its care*

The crying baby girl arrives at the Foundling Hospital wrapped in a few tattered rags. She is not yet two months old. Nobody remembers who left her in the basket hung on the gate in Guildford Street. The only clue is a scrap of paper with a message penned in ink: 'This infant has no father and the mother lame and miserably poor and has had nothing to keep it but of Brest.' The note adds that the girl's name is Mary Somervill. It will not be her name for much longer. Mary will be taken to the chapel and baptised under a new name, Sarah Elton. Then she and fourteen other babies will be transported to wet nurses in the cleaner air of Brentwood in Essex. She will survive another five months before succumbing to measles.

Sarah Elton is the 95th baby left at the Foundling Hospital today, 2 June 1756. It is the first day of a new scheme funded by the Government at a cost of £10,000. Advertisements have been placed in newspapers announcing that the hospital will take in all unwanted babies for the next six months, no questions asked. It may be that they are illegitimate children who would bring shame on their mothers. It may be their parents are too poor or too ill to cope. That does not matter. The hospital will accept them all, providing they are free from disease and under two months old.

The hospital prepared by recruiting 140 extra nurses living out in the country; in Enfield and Edmonton to the north of the capital; in Woodford, Brentwood and Romford in Essex to the east; in Hanwell,

Heston and Hillingdon in Middlesex, Midgham and Newbury in Berkshire and St Peter's Chalfont in Buckinghamshire to the west; and Epsom in Surrey and Barham and Bromley in Kent to the south. It also ordered in a huge amount of clothing, to allow each child to have four caps, four long stays, four neckcloths, four shirts and twelve clouts (undergarments), a grey linsey mantle, two white blankets, two swaddling bands, a grey linsey coat and a petticoat.

Yet it is unlikely anyone at the hospital expected how many children it would receive on the first day. Over the previous 15 years it has taken in less than 1,400 children. Today it will receive a total of 117, at a rate of one every five minutes. The delivery of so many babies has naturally attracted a crowd outside in the street. Some of the people here are mothers begging for their child back. Others have discovered that their errant partner has delivered their baby to the hospital in their absence. Some people are here just to observe the spectacle.

Meanwhile the staff follows a set procedure. Each child has to be given a number. This number, together with the estimated age of the baby and the items of clothing it arrived in, are recorded on a pre-printed sheet of paper. In some cases the warden notes down which parish the child came from, whether it has been baptised and any name it has been given. Any items left with the baby are folded up within the piece of paper.

Child 1401 arrives with a note reading simply 'Lydia'.

Child 1405 arrives with a note reading 'The bearer hereof is Richard Pearce'.

Child 1409 arrives with a note reading 'Born March 25 1756 baptised Robert Wood be pleased not to alter the name of the child its parents being lawful married and of a good family but at present in great distress.'

Child 1435 arrives with a note reading 'You are desired to christen this child by the name of Mary Phillips to take care of the things it comes in that the parents may as soon as able fetch it out again.'

None of these children will keep their given name. All are taken to the chapel and given new identities before being sent off to their wet or dry nurses. They are often named after famous people in English history. So Child 1403, named John Thomson by his parents, becomes Henry Tudor, while Child 1409 (Robert Wood) becomes Roger Bacon.

Some parents leave tokens with the children, perhaps so they can be identified and reclaimed later. These range from lottery tickets to jewellery.

Child 1416 arrives with a box containing a silver coin and bits of wood.

Child 1440 arrives with a piece of blue ribbon and a note reading 'This child has been publicly christened by the name of Elias Norman.'

Child 1489 arrives with a piece of white and green striped cotton.

Child 1495 arrives with a piece of paper bearing a wax seal displaying a coat of arms and a message, written in a fine hand, claiming that the father is away at sea.

Many of the children arrive with nothing.

Some of the children come from richer districts of London like Hanover Square or Hyde Park. Others come from the poorest parts such as Ratcliffe Highway and Whitechapel. One girl arrives with a note stating she came from Bury St Edmunds. Child 1419 is brought to the hospital from the Bethnal Green workhouse by the parish overseer along with a note stating she is 'exposed and deserted . . . and nursed at the expense of the parish'.

Two babies, both girls, arrive in such poor health that they are taken straight to the infirmary. Child 1497, from Whitechapel in the East End, will die in thirteen days. Child 1498, from the parish of St Giles, will make it to a dry nurse in Epsom but will die on 20 May 1757.

Of the 117 children received on this day, nearly half will die by the end of the year. This staggering death toll is normal for London, where mortality rates are often double that of anywhere else in the country thanks to filthy living conditions and the spread of disease. It is part of the reason why a gentleman named Thomas Coram came up with the idea for the Foundling Hospital in 1735. With the support of aristocratic ladies including the Duchess of Somerset, he handed in a petition to George II arguing that something should be done about the number of abandoned infants in the capital of England. 'No expedient has yet been found out for the preventing the frequent murders of poor miserable infants at their birth, or for suppressing the inhuman custom of exposing new born infants to perish in the street, or putting out such unhappy foundlings to wicked and barbarous nurses, who undertake to bring them up for a small and trifling sum of money, too often suffer them to starve for the want of due sustenance or care, or if permitted to live, either turn them into the streets to beg or steal, or hire them out to loose persons.' Four years later the King signed a Royal Charter for the establishment of hospital for deserted children. When the hospital began in 1741 it took in children under two years old but places were limited because of a lack of funding. The new building in Bloomsbury opened in 1745.

Not everybody agrees that the hospital is a good thing. Dr Samuel Johnson criticised the lack of religious education, believing the children were destined to hang from the gallows as criminals. Others claimed that the hospital encouraged loose morals among women who no longer had to fear becoming pregnant. It is even suggested that people have been paid to bring in children from all over the country, only to get rid of them along the way.

Despite these allegations the hospital has attracted the support of the composer Handel and the artist William Hogarth (a founding governor). The philanthropist Jonas Hanway estimates that every life saved by the hospital represents a profit of more than £176 by the age of fifty.

So what happens to the foundlings that survive the dangerous early stages of life? They will be returned by the wet nurses either to the hospital or to one of its branches (including Shrewsbury and Ackworth in Yorkshire). They will be given a uniform of brown Yorkshire serge with a slip of red cloth across the shoulder and white hats with a red binding. They will be taught to read and write and put to work in the hospital, fuelled by three meals a day: a breakfast of bread and butter or porridge, a dinner of beef and potatoes or mutton and greens and a supper of porridge or bread and cheese.

Perhaps a third of the children will make it to the age of apprenticeship (usually between 10 and 14). They will be sent off to a master or mistress and taught a trade until they are at least 21 years old.

Child 1385 will be packed off to a gentleman in Bridlington in the County of York as a husbandry apprentice at the age of 13.

Child 1387 will be sent to Walworth in south London at the age of 17 to work as a lace or tambour maker.

Child 1466 will be placed with an exchange broker in Surrey at the age of nine to be employed in household work. The apprenticeship will pay £5 a year until he reaches the age of 23.

Only one child will be returned to its parents. This boy, named by the hospital as Henry Long, will be delivered to his father at the age of eight on 23 May 1764.

The hospital received another forty-three children the following day, 3 June 1756. By the end of the first week a total of 299 children had passed through its doors. The scheme was later extended for another six months and continued until 1760. By then nearly the hospital had taken in nearly 15,000 children at a cost of £500,000. Only 4,400 of those survived to go into apprenticeship. Despite losing Government funding the hospital continued to take in children throughout the eighteenth and nineteenth centuries, attracting the support of the author Charles Dickens. It moved to Berkhamsted in Hertfordshire in the 1920s and the building in Bloomsbury was demolished.

CHAPTER 16

Night Walkers

*In which we observe the treatment of prostitutes in
eighteenth-century Georgian London*

On a hot Thursday night in July 1742 Mary Maurice and her cousin
Sarah Bland are working as prostitutes in St Martin's Lane, half way
between Leicester Square and Covent Garden. They are not the only
'night walkers' about at this time – 11pm is the hour when the 'publick
streets begin to swarm with whores and pickpockets' while the rest of
the city drifts off to sleep. Estimates of their numbers vary from 3,000
to 80,000 and some gentlemen complain of being accosted by 100
lewd, winking women in just one mile's walk along the Strand. Some
of the girls offering their services are just eight or nine years old. Then
there are the harlots 'exposing themselves at the windows and doors
of bawdy-houses, like beasts in a market for publick sale'.

Mary Maurice is what you would call a casual prostitute, a
working-class married woman hoping to earn a bit of extra money at
the end of the day. She is of 'middling size' but suffers slightly from
dropsy, perhaps because of her poor diet and taste for Gin. Her outfit
– a black petticoat, a long, white gown, and bright red shoes – is
designed to attract attention. Unfortunately for her, the attention comes
from the parish constables who have been given specific orders to clear
the streets. Mary and Sarah are among twenty women and eight men
seized that night and taken down the road to an unofficial prison
known as St Martin's Roundhouse to await their appearance before a
Magistrate the next morning. Some of them may be well known
criminals or troublemakers, but others appear to have simply been in
the wrong place at the wrong time.

The cousins are led past a set of stocks and up four stone steps into a kind of reception room. Several other women are already here, talking, smoking tobacco and drinking beer and whisky provided (for a fee) by the Roundhouse keeper's wife. Mary and Sarah are either unwilling or unable to pay and are soon hustled through a locked wooden door and down a set of stairs to a cell on the lower-ground floor known as 'The Hole'. It is roughly six foot high and six foot six inches long by six foot two inches wide. There are wooden benches along the walls for the prisoners to sit on and a small iron-barred window set in the far wall. With perhaps a dozen women already here, the Hole is already starting to feel unbearably hot. Added to that is a terrible smell emanating from the sewer running directly beneath the building. Mary and Sarah manage to find a space on one of the benches and sit down to wait until the morning.

Also in the cell are Mary Cosier, who was picked up in a cook-shop, Sarah Starkes and Ann Branch, a crooked old woman in a red cloak. By 1am they are all sweating profusely in the enclosed space and still air and many of the women begin to strip off in an attempt to keep cool. One or two cry out for water, Gin or wine to quench their thirst. They are ignored.

Between two and three o'clock in the morning the keeper William Bird sends another group of women down to the hole from the waiting room. One of them is Phyllis Wells, a young girl in a light brown camlet dress, who claims she was up to nothing more sinister than walking to her brother-in-law's home in Covent Garden with the medicinal herb coltsfoot. Another is Elizabeth Amey, a waitress at Mr Eastmead's bagnio (a brothel masquerading as a bath house). Mary Cosier takes the opportunity to beg William Bird for water: 'For Christ's sake let us have Water, for the Lord's sake a little water, for we are stifled with heat.' Some of the women, cramped up together on the benches, are feeling faint. One or two have stripped completely naked. William Bird ignores their pleas: 'Damn the bitches, they just want Gin.'

When he returns an hour or so later with yet more prisoners, Mary Maurice begs to be let out: 'For God's sake Mr Bird let us have some

Air or some Water to relieve us, or take some of us away, and put us in another place.' Others cry out 'Fire' and tell Mr Bird that one of the women is in labour. Ann Cosier offers a shilling for half an hour in the open air. Elizabeth Amey demands to be let out to pay her 'reckoning' and starts screaming that the cell is like an oven. There is a short struggle, Bird's candle falls to the floor and Amey's cap is knocked off.

Angrily, Bird shouts: 'Damn you, you bitch, for your sake all shall suffer.'

By 5am there are already 20 women in the Hole when Bird orders the beadle to take down another three, including Elizabeth Surridge, who had fallen asleep by the fireside upstairs. The beadle refuses, insisting there is not enough room. 'If you put them in you will stifle them.' Bird rushes down with a long staff in his hand and physically forces the women into the room before closing the door.

The situation inside the Hole is now desperate. Every minute seems like an hour. Mary Maurice slumps down from the bench, her head resting on her cousin's knee. 'Cousin let me die,' she sighs, 'let me die for God's sake.' With that she slips down to the floor and into darkness. Several women gather at the window to beg for help from passers-by and ask for their landladies and mistresses to be told of their arrest. Money is offered to Mr Bird for their freedom, or a glass of water, but he insists it is impossible. A few minutes later he spots somebody trying to pass a quartern of Gin through the grate and angrily knocks the cup to the floor. He then padlocks the wooden shutter closed, telling the women inside: 'Now you bitches you shall not have the window opened but die and be damned.'

The women shout 'Murder! Murder!'.

One of them takes of her shoe and bangs it repeatedly on the ceiling.

Elizabeth Surridge, racked with thirst, has an idea. She sends some of the people outside the shutters to fetch a tobacco pipe and some beer from the alehouse. The small ends of the pipes are inserted through the slits in the shutters so that the beer can be poured into the prisoners' waiting mouths. But only two women are able to take advantage of the cunning plan before William Bird's son pushes the Good Samaritan away and breaks the pipe.

At 7am William Bird retires to bed.

Inside the cell Mary Cosier's handkerchief is so drenched with sweat it has gone stiff. The woman next to her, Ann Branch, slumps down dead. Several others are already lying on the floor, their limbs and faces discoloured. Still the door remains shut.

At 8am the warrant has still not returned from the Magistrate.

Two more hours pass.

Finally at 10am William Bird gets out of bed and opens the shutters on the window. Elizabeth Surridge holds up the arm of one of her fellow prisoners and tells him: 'Here is one woman dead, and the rest are a dying.' He does not reply.

The door opens and several women tumble out on to the beadle William Anderson. The nauseating smell strikes him with similar force. The women cry out for water. Elizabeth Sturridge finds a pint of dirty water and drinks it down in one go. She begs Mrs Bird for more: 'For God Almighty's sake, give me a little water, for I am almost perished.' Mary Cosier pours the contents of a tea kettle down her throat before promptly vomiting it back up again. A surgeon arrives to find Ann Branch and Mary Maurice already dead, their faces bloated and their skin black with stagnant blood. Three others are having fits inside the Hole. He puts one in a chair and gives her wine and water. He bleeds Phyllis Wells in an attempt to save her life but she dies half an hour later. Others are taken to the workhouse infirmary. Only thirteen of them are fit enough to be taken to Bow Street. They are all allowed to go free after the Magistrate is told that some of the prisoners have died.

Outside St Martin's Roundhouse, an angry mob gathers, intent on pulling it to the ground.

* * *

On the morning of 2 May 1758 a group of twenty-five prostitutes arrested at the bawdy houses of Covent Garden are brought before Sir

John Fielding, the blind Magistrate of Bow Street. They are all aged between 15 and 22, their 'sweetest features disguised by dirt and filth'. Many are orphans left to roam the streets. Others claim their fathers are at sea or have run away. Only two have decided to leave their parents in the country and head for the city. In Sir John's opinion, they often come from the families of labourers and servants 'whose families are generally too large to receive maintenance much less education from the labour of their parents, and the lives of their fathers being often shortened by their intemperance'. Many of them have been involved in prostitution for a year or more – indeed one 16-year-old claims to have started aged 12. Some have already been treated for sexually transmitted diseases with doses of mercury, which can cause patients to produce excessive saliva. 'Many of them are now foul', Sir John records. As he looks once more at the girls standing before him – three aged 15, four aged 16, one aged 17, five aged 18, six aged 19, three aged 20, two aged 21 and one aged 22 – Sir John decides that something must be done to remove these poor orphaned girls from the streets without simply sending them to Bridewell for a whipping and a short term of imprisonment.

His plan is to establish a public laundry or reformatory to employ 'the deserted girls of the poor of this metropolis, and also to reform those prostitutes whom necessity has drove into the streets, and who are willing to return to virtue and obtain an honest livelihood by severe industry.' These young women will be taught a trade and freed from the desperation that forces them on to the streets.

The Lambeth Asylum for Orphaned Girls, as it will become known, is to admit girls from the age of nine as long as they are free of disease. Another project, supported by the philanthropist Jonas Hanway, is the Magdalen Hospital for the Reception of Penitent Prostitutes (under the age of 30), to be set up in Whitechapel in the East End. Together, it is hoped, they will turn whores into housewives, or as Hanway describes it 'a work of creation as well as redemption'.

Not everybody is impressed by their endeavours. One writer, styling himself a 'reformed rake', publishes a leaflet in response to Fielding's plan pointing out that prostitutes – otherwise known as

Cyprians, impures, strumpets, light girls, thaises, wantons, jades, hussies, tarts, nymphs, jezebels, doxies, molls, trollopes and harlots – are not all poor, abandoned waifs selling themselves on the street. He claims that we could also include aristocratic 'women of fashion who intrigue', high-born 'demi-reps' who have affairs, 'kept mistresses' who are funded by married men and 'ladies of pleasure' who work in high-class brothels. Then below them are the 'common' whores who hang out in taverns, coffee houses, theatres and bawdy houses, the street walkers and park walkers. At the bottom are the bunters and the bulkmongers, so called because they sleep on the 'bulks' below shop windows.

The Reformed Rake believes that the sight of a kept mistress riding around in style in her chariot is more likely to corrupt us than the 'miserable street walker who perhaps has not rags enough to cover her nakedness'. Some prostitutes are celebrities: Fanny Murray, the inspiration for the main character in the novel *Fanny Hill* (1748), overcame the loss of her parents at the age of 12 and within five years was one of the most famous (and fashionable) figures in London. Fanny had only to change her cap or dress and soon every woman in the city was clamouring for the same outfit. It is rumoured the actress Lavinia Fenton, who is married to the Duke of Bolton, was put to work as a child prostitute by her own mother (who sold her virginity for £200) before she found fame as an actress.

Then there are the women immortalised in Harris' *List of Covent Garden Ladies*, first published in 1757. In its pages you might find Lucy Paterson, a prostitute said to work in St Martin's Lane. Her father died in Newgate Prison and she is regularly sent to Bridewell for punishment. 'She is not pretty, neither ugly, but is as lewd as goats and monkeys, and she generally has a design upon her freind's watch purse of handkerchief. She . . . is in a homely phrase, a vile bitch.' Or Pol Forrester, said to work in Bow Street. 'She has an entrance to the palace of pleasure as wide as a church door, and a breath worse than a welch bagpipe. She drinks like a fish, eats like a horse, and swears like a trooper – an errant drab.'

* * *

It is King George III's 25th birthday, 4 June 1763, and the Scottish lawyer James Boswell is determined to celebrate in style. He dresses himself in his 'second mourning suit', a dark, shabby outfit complimented with dirty buckskin breeches, black stockings and a round hat with tarnished silver lace. He grabs an old oaken stick to pound upon the pavement and sets off for St James' Park to pick up a prostitute while in the guise of a 'blackguard'.

Boswell's first choice is a 'low Brimstone' (poor, deserted, aged) who agrees to go with him to a secluded spot in return for a mere sixpence. On the way he gets out his 'machine', a condom fashioned from sheep's intestines, and dips it into the canal. Now protected from sexual disease, he sets to work. In his opinion, he performs 'most manfully'.

In a state of some euphoria he tramps from St James' to St Paul's and downs three bowls of liquor at Ashley's Punch-house on Ludgate Hill. Still unsatisfied, he approaches 'a little profligate wretch' on the Strand and gives her sixpence. She attempts to get away before he is finished. He grabs her roughly and pushes her against the wall but she wriggles away and screams out for help. Her cries attract other prostitutes and a group of soldiers but Boswell manages to persuade him that the girl is in the wrong. 'Brother Soldiers,' he says, 'Should not a halfpay officer roger for sixpence? And here has she used me so and so.' After showering her with insults he walks away in the direction of Whitehall, where he quickly finds another girl to his liking. This time he boasts he is a highwayman, hoping she will let him have his way with her for free. She sees through his disguise, however; a drunkard and a rogue he may be, but he will always remain a Gentleman. Boswell returns home at two o'clock in the morning, tired but satisfied.

William Bird was convicted of the murder of Phyllis Wells after two trials at the Old Bailey. He was spared hanging and sentenced to transportation to America for life. Ironically, during the voyage across the Atlantic he was starved of food and water by the ship's commander and died before reaching the coast of Maryland.

The Lambeth Asylum for Orphaned Girls was rebuilt in 1824 before moving to Beddington in Surrey and then High Wycombe in Buckinghamshire. The Magdalen Hospital relocated first to Bayswater and then Streatham before becoming an 'Approved School for Female Offenders' in 1934. The school closed in 1966.

James Boswell survived until 1795 despite contracting venereal diseases at least seventeen times. He is now most famous as the biographer and friend of the lexicographer Samuel Johnson.

CHAPTER 17

The Black Poor

*In which we meet the Black Poor of London in 1815
and recall the remarkable scheme to relocate them to
Africa thirty years earlier*

Outside the Adelphi Theatre in London's West End a crowd gathers to watch the latest performance of the famous 'one-legged musical negro'. Billy Waters stands before them in a ragged uniform topped off with a cocked hat decked with ribbons and feathers. In his left hand he clutches a battered violin. Then, with a sudden kick of his wooden leg, he tucks the violin beneath his chin begins to play. 'Kitty will you marry me, Kitty will you cry,' he sings, 'Kitty will you marry me, Kitty will you cry! cry-cry!' Each kick of his wooden leg is met with laughter, applause and the clatter of pennies into his collection tin.

Billy is one of an estimated 15,000 people of African origin now living in England (total population nine million in 1801). He claims to have been born in America and says he lost his leg falling from the rigging of HMS *Ganymede* under the command of Sir John Purvis. Once in London he determined to make what he called 'an honest living by scraping de cat-gut'. Like the other so-called 'St Giles blackbirds' (after the poor parish of St Giles where they live), he is unable to claim poor relief because he is not settled resident and cannot be sent back overseas. Another blackbird, Master Toby, is a familiar sight in the area because of his habit of walking almost bent over double using two crutches attached to his hands. He also wears a white handkerchief around his head and is fond of spending whatever money he obtains begging on Gin.

111

The elderly Jamaican Charles McGee (born 1744) occupies his post at the Obelisk in the middle of the crossroads at the bottom of Ludgate Hill. It is a prime location for begging given the thousands of people who walk past him every day. Charles is also hard to miss, with his one eye, his woolly grey hair and smart coat.

Then there is Joseph Johnson, an unemployed merchant seaman who varies his pitch in order to outwit the parish beadles attempting to remove him from the streets and set him to work on the treadmill. One of his acts involves wearing a model of the ship *Nelson* upon his cap while singing 'The Storm' by George Alexander Stevens, bending his head to mimic the motion of the waves:

Cease, rude Boreas, blust'ring railer!
List, ye landsmen, all to me;
Messmates, hear a brother sailor
Sing the dangers of the sea;
From bounding billows first in motion,
When the distant whirlwinds rise,
To the tempest-troubled ocean,
Where the seas contend with skies.

The history of black people in England is said to begin in 1555 when five slaves were brought here from West Africa. Seven years later Sir John Hawkins made his first slave trading expedition and by the late seventeenth century slaves were freely bought and sold in the ports of London and Liverpool. One advertisement in 1756 offered a 'Negro Boy, about fourteen years old, warranted free from any distemper' for £25. Black servants were employed by George I and Samuel Pepys, and it became fashionable for the aristocracy to take young black boys with them to the theatre and other social occasions, almost as if they were pets. The Duchess of Kingston, Elizabeth Chudleigh, kept a black boy named Sambo until the age of 18 or 19 when he was returned to slavery in the West Indies. This trend was already in decline when in 1772 Lord Mansfield ruled that black slaves could not be forcibly removed from England. Many believed that this judgement effectively freed all slaves in this country, but there is no law specifically banning it.

Larger numbers of black people came here after the American colonies gained their independence. Many of them fought with the British Navy after being promised their freedom and decided to settle in England rather than Canada or another parts of the British Empire. But while some were able to claim compensation, others were left to 'shift for themselves'. This, at a time of few available jobs, was no easy thing. By the winter of 1785/6 it was common to see the 'Black Poor', as they became known, begging on the streets of London. Their plight led to a group of philanthropic gentlemen organising a collection of money and food for their relief. This group became known as 'The Committee for the Relief of the Black Poor'.

At first its efforts extended to food – in January 1786 it placed an advertisement offering a small loaf to 'every distressed black' who turned up at a baker's shop in Cavendish Square in the West End of London the following Saturday. Donations to the committee quickly reached £428 within a month thanks to the support of the 'benevolent Nobility and Gentry' including the Duchess of Devonshire, the Countess of Essex and the Marchioness of Buckingham. It was a popular cause, not least because it was felt Britain owed them for their support during the war. 'They ought at least to be warmly clothed, considering the heat of their native climate,' noted one observer, 'whereas these wretched mendicants are in rags.'

The committee hired rooms in two public houses in Mile End, in east London, and Marylebone in the west, to dish out broth, a piece of meat and a twopenny loaf to every applicant. A makeshift hospital was also established in Warren Street. Soon more than 200 of the Black Poor were receiving relief every day. Some were provided with clothes, bedding and shoes and provided with a place to sleep. Others were given help finding jobs or transport to Canada where there was more opportunity for employment.

By April the government had become involved in the relief effort and it was decided that the Black Poor should be given a flat allowance of six pence a day. More than 300 men, women and children were taking advantage of the payments by May 1786 but this was seen as only a short-term solution. The answer, it was decided, was to fund

113

the settlement of the Black Poor in a place more 'congenial to their constitutions'. The country chosen was Sierra Leone.

This proposal was not universally welcomed by the Black Poor receiving daily relief, as some of them preferred to return to America or the West Indies. Others asked for signed 'Instrument' guaranteeing their freedom if they agreed to go. Yet by October a total of 675 had been won round to the scheme and certificates were drawn up describing the holder as 'a freeman of the colony of Sierra Leona'. Even then they were slow to embark upon the ships hired to take them to Africa and perhaps as many as sixty died before they left England. It was not until 9 April 1787 that the expedition set sail from Plymouth with 409 passengers. Although most were black men, there were also fifty-nine white women, forty-one black women and several children. One of the white women was Sarah Whitecuffe, the widow of Benjamin Whitecuffe, a former loyalist soldier who narrowly escaped being hanged by American forces in New Jersey and eventually arrived in London in 1783 to marry an English wife and set himself up as a saddler and chaircaner.

The Sierra Leone scheme was not a success. Thirty-five of the passengers died during the voyage and those that made it to the 'Land of Freedom' were decimated by disease. Only sixty of the original settlers were still alive when they were joined by another 1,200 African-Americans from Nova Scotia in 1792.

Billy Waters was caricatured by George Cruikshank in 1819 and went on to star in the theatrical production of 'Tom and Jerry' *at the Adelphi in 1821. He died two years later in St Giles Workhouse, shortly after being elected 'King of the Beggars'. Slavery was abolished across most of the British Empire in 1834.*

CHAPTER 18

Poor Stockingers

In which we meet the frame-workers of Nottingham and Leicester between 1812 and 1819 as they struggle to make a living at a time of war, rioting and economic depression

Thomas Daykin has been a framework knitter in Mount Sorrell in Nottinghamshire since 1775. God knows how many stockings he has turned out on the complex hand-and-foot-operated machines in the last forty-four years. God knows how many hours he has spent at his craft just to earn the 14 or 15 shillings a week he needs to feed his family. It has never been a handsomely-rewarded trade but it has provided a relatively comfortable living for thousands of men, women and children across the Midlands counties for generations.

Not any more it seems. Like many knitters, Mr Daykin struggles to make half what he did even four or five years ago and has to rely on his wife and six children (aged from four to 16) to make up some of the difference. 'I cannot earn more than six shillings a week if I work six days in the week from six in the morning till eleven at night,' he tells us. 'I have four children that cannot get me a shilling a week. I believe that the whole earnings of my family are about 13 shillings a week.'

So desperate are his circumstances that for the last two years he has received three shillings a week from the parish authorities in Nottingham to top up his wages. He is perhaps a little embarrassed about this, as he quickly points out that he has paid the poor rates in Mount Sorrell for the past sixteen years.

William Jackson, a framework knitter from Leicester, has been unable to pay the rates for the last six months because of the reduction in his wages. He reckons that he could earn 14 shillings a week in 1811 before the industry started to run into trouble. Now he cannot get more than eight shillings a week. By putting his wife and three of his six children to work the family receives perhaps 18 shillings and sixpence a week. It is not enough to live on any more. 'Our expenditure exceeds our income and at this time I owe three quarters rent and a half year's taxes,' he says. 'I have sold a frame to live upon and parted with several necessaries out of my house besides.'

Still, it could be worse. Mr Jackson knows other knitters who survive on little more than bread and water because they are unable to apply to a parish. 'There are many who have not had flesh meat perhaps once in two months,' he says. 'The general way of living is upon roots and water gruel.'

The reliance of frameworkers on poor relief appears to be widespread across Leicestershire. In Wickston Magna, according to Thomas Measures, a knitter for thirty-four years, there are as many as 248 families receiving aid. Still more are unable to earn enough to maintain their families even when in full-time work. In the parish of St Margaret's in Leicester itself there are twenty-four unemployed men claiming a total of 100s a week, thirty-six part-timers claiming a total of 103s and sixty-one in full-time work claiming a total of 300s.

So why is this happening? Framework knitting is after all a skilled job that has long been at the heart of England's textile industry, producing silk, lace and cotton stockings, hose, gloves, shirts and shawls. The stocking frame was invented in Calverton outside Nottingham in 1589 and by 1812 there were perhaps 25,000 frames in use nationwide. In Nottingham alone, a town of some 30,000 people, there were 2,600.

These machines, bristling with many different parts, are not straightforward to operate but give the user a huge advantage over the hand knitter. By deploying various moving parts, including the needles, jacks, sinkers, the presser, the neb, the copens and the slur, the framework can make 6,000 loops of yarn a minute compared to the 100 loops a minute achieved by older methods. The newest versions are also extremely expensive and as a result most knitters have to rent them from their masters, the hosiers. This fee, which is taken out of their wages, is one of the many grievances of the impoverished frame-worker. Other deductions are made for candles, extra equipment and any supposed defects in the finished product. All of which makes it even more difficult for the knitter to earn a living.

Thomas Latham, from Nottingham, tells us the story how one hosier refused to pay him for a pair of perfectly good stockings. 'As he was examining the hose he stuck his pen in his hair, and as he tucked the pen in a blot of ink fell upon one of the hose,' he explains. 'Then he took up the other hose and after a minute examination for ten minutes, perhaps to find something to find fault with, because he had spoilt them, he then found what we call a twist, which requires a thread being run through it to make it perfect and sound . . . but the thread not being quite so clean as the stocking he observed it and said it was a mended stocking. "Oh," says he, "you need not bring your mended stockings here, if I could sell your old mended stockings I could sell all my old stockings," and he refused to take them. I remarked that I saw the ink drop, which he did not deny, but he still refused to take them.'

Another complaint is that the masters pay the knitters in goods rather than money. Mr Latham remembers a man who spent two weeks making a piece of lace worth £2 8s and was paid with a piece of woollen cloth capable of being made into a coat. 'The man at that time wanting money more than a coat, was induced to sell it as soon as possible,' he says. 'After offering it for sale and many places he at last found a customer who gave him 10s 6d for the whole.' Other knitters have been paid in sugar, shoes, herrings, vegetables, bacon and cheese. In many cases the frame-worker is forced to buy his food and other necessities from a shop owned by his master, and at inflated prices. This practice of 'payment in kind' is so rife that some communities run on it. As Edward Allen of Sutton-in-Ashfield explains: 'It has been so common in our town to pay goods instead of money that a number of my neighbours have been obliged to pay sugar for drugs out of the druggist's shop, and others have been obliged to pay sugar for drapery goods and such things. I was credibly informed that one person paid half a pound of sugar and a penny to have a tooth drawn, and a neighbour of mine told me that he had heard the sexton had been paid for digging a grave with sugar and tea.'

The workers are banned from forming trade unions to pressure their masters into paying higher wages, thanks to the Combination Act of 1799. So it is perhaps not surprising that the anger of the framework knitters at the low wages and lack of work eventually erupted into violence. On 11 March 1811 there was a protest by as many as 1,000 stockingers in the marketplace of Nottingham. The Dragoon Guards were called out but nothing happened until later that evening when a large crowd of 200 or 300 men marched north to the town of Arnold and set about destroying the knitting frames owned by the hosiers they blamed for their troubles. A total of sixty-three frames were destroyed that night. Within days the riots had spread to Sutton in Ashfield and other county towns and a reward of £50 was offered for help catching the frame-breakers:

> WHEREAS several EVIL-MINDED PERSONS have assembled together in riotous Manner, and DESTROYED a NUMBER of FRAMES In different Parts of the Country: THIS IS TO GIVE NOTICE That any Person who will give Information of any Person or Persons thus wickedly BREAKING THE FRAMES Shall, upon CONVICTION, receive 50 GUINEAS REWARD And any Person who was actively engaged in RIOTING, who will impach his Accomplices, shall, upon CONVICTION, receive the same Reward, and every Effort made to procure his Pardon.

After a lull during the summer months, frame-breaking started up again in November, accompanied by threatening letters signed with the name 'Ludd'. In the New Year the Luddites issued their declaration of war:

> We do hereby declare to all Hosiers, lace manufacturers and proprietors of frames that we will break and destroy all manner of

frames whatsoever that make the following spurious articles and all frames soever that do not pay the regular prices heretofore agreed to by the masters and workmen.

When the attacks spread to Derbyshire, Leicestershire and Yorkshire, Parliament took action on 1 March 1812 by passing a Bill making frame-breaking a hanging offence. The poet Lord Byron was the most notable figure to oppose the new law, telling the assembled peers that 'it cannot be denied that they have arisen from circumstances of the most unparalleled distress . . . nothing but absolute want could have driven a large, and once honest and industrious, body of the people into the commission of excesses so hazardous to themselves, their families and the community'.

The following month hundreds of Luddites launched an attack on Rawfold's mill in Liversedge in the West Riding of Yorkshire only to be driven back by gunfire from the owner's hired militia. A few weeks later another mill owner was shot dead near Huddersfield after vowing to 'ride up to his saddle in Luddite blood'. Three men were hanged for his murder and another fourteen were executed for their role in other violence following a series of trials in York in January 1813. Although disturbances continued until around 1817, the Luddite rebellion was over.

Although Parliament attempted to investigate whether anything could be done to help the framework knitters, their situation did not improve. John Thorpe, a Leicester man who has been in the trade for thirty-five years, tells us that it has been getting worse 'for eight or ten years'. He adds: 'At that time we were able to earn on the average about 13 to 15 shillings a week. We are now not able to earn more than seven to eight shillings a week and in many instances not more than six.' He says he earns that eight shillings for fifteen hours work a day, six days a week. 'Some days I work twenty hours,' he says. 'If I have no employment one day, I must make it up another.' He estimates that 3,000 of the 14,000 frameworkers in Leicestershire have lost their jobs and now rely on parish relief. 'Their parishes are overburthened to such an extent as they never before experienced. Whole rows of houses that that used to contribute to the parish funds are now under the necessity of receiving relief.'

But what are the causes of the decline in wages? Some framework knitters say that the industry was damaged by the decision to restrict trade with America before the War of 1812. But their real hostility is reserved for the growth in cheaper, lower-quality gloves and stockings which can be produced in greater quantities by lower-skilled workers. The result, they claim, is job losses, lower wages and the destruction of an entire industry.

Just ask Thomas Latham: 'The principal causes of the distress as I imagine are the introduction of bad and fraudulent work which has brought the trade into disrepute and consequently lessened the sale of those articles in the markets.' He claims that the lace industry was hit particularly badly, throwing more than 1,000 hands out of work. The unemployed instead turned to the other branches of the textile industry, silk and cotton. 'The hosiers took the advantage of this and brought on more alarming impositions upon the workmen,' he adds. Workers are now required to work harder and longer for the same wages. 'I believe it is entirely owing to this the present depressed state of our manufactures.'

John Blackneer, a framework knitter in Nottingham since 1780, agrees. In particular, he blames what are known as 'cut-ups', articles that are cut out from a single piece of fabric made on a wider frame. Whereas the best stockings cost three shillings a dozen, the cut-ups are half that. 'It throws a part of the men out of employment, and it is not of advantage to the state or the country at large because by men being thus driven from their labour and the same quantity of goods being still made by fewer hands these goods disgrace themselves by their manufacture.' He is so convinced that cut-ups are to blame that he wants the Government to ban them. 'It is my opinion that if the stockings were prohibited from being cut out from pieces that it would have a tendency to restore the character of every branch of the trade that has been lost.'

The younger, lower-skilled workers who make these cheaper stockings are known in the trade as 'colts'. Unlike the children of established framework knitters they have not served an apprenticeship. Their stockings can be sold at a cheaper price to customers who are unable to tell the difference (it is only when washed that the cheaper one falls to pieces, say the knitters). Lower prices paid for stockings inevitably result in lower wages as the hosiers struggle to stay in business.

There are other problems too, that make this a perfect storm for the framework knitting industry. Prices for silk and wool remain high and fashion is changing. It appears respectable gentlemen are no longer flocking to the market to spend 25 shillings a time on silk stockings. As the hosier James Hooley explains: 'Coloured stockings of every description have gone out of fashion. There is a fashion, which cause I know not, makes a thing come into demand today and tomorrow it cannot be sold. About the same period that these things were very much in demand, ribbed hose were so much in demand that we could not make enough of them. Now the same article is positively made better than I ever knew the but we have no demand for them.'

The fashionable people now prefer to wear boots and gaiters instead.

The domestic frame-work knitting industry continued to decline and in 1845 it was noted that many of the knitters were living in poverty in sparsely-furnished rooms in city slums. However, some hand-operated frames remained in use in the twentieth century despite the introduction of steam-powered machines.

CHAPTER 19

The Workhouse

*In which we witness the terrible conditions at the Andover Union
in Hampshire in 1845, one of the workhouses established
under the New Poor Law*

Bones are delivered to the workhouse three times a week. There are beef bones, mutton bones, bacon bones and horse bones. Perhaps there are even human bones stolen from graveyards. They have been scavenged from all over the parish and sold to the workhouse to be crushed into dust by the pauper inmates. This bone dust can then be sold to local farmers as fertiliser for a profit.

The ragged group of men gathered in the yard today are not interested in profit. They have their eyes fixed on the bones being tipped out on to the ground. Not because they are eager to start work, but because they are looking for a certain type of bone. A fresh bone, perhaps with a few sinews of muscle still attached. A fresh bone full of tasty, nourishing marrow.

All at once a cry goes up. Three men dash for the same mutton bone, so fresh that it looks like it has just fallen from a nobleman's table. Two of them reach it at the same time and scuffle on the dirty ground, each one trying to prise it away from the other's grip. One man wins, and takes the bone away to hide it somewhere so he can enjoy it later when noone is looking. The other men poke around in the hope of finding ones nearly as fresh. Some are so hungry they pick up a stale, rotting bone, or a sheep's head. One of the paupers, a man named Reeves who is generally referred to as an 'idiot', is famous for eating from the bones that everybody else shies away from in disgust.

There he is now, gnawing on a hairy horse's leg in the corner of the yard.

We ask a few inmates if this is what usually happens when the men arrive for bone-crushing work. George Petty, who lives at home but comes to the Andover Union to work for food and a shilling in cash, is not ashamed to admit it. 'I have eaten the marrow from the bones myself. Almost all the inmates eat the marrow. If there is a beef shin bone we break it and suck it, but we never do that unless the bone is fresh – I know the bone is fresh by the smell.' Charles Coombs has lived at the workhouse with his wife and five children since Easter. He tells us: 'When the marrow is fresh and good most of us eat it. Sometimes a bone comes in fresh and we eat the meat. But here and there one man fancies the marrow from the stale bones.'

The most explicit is Samuel Green, a father of five grown-up children who has been here since the New Year. 'We look out for the fresh bones and when a fresh bone comes in we are like a parcel of dogs after them. Bacon marrow bones are good. I have picked a sheep's head, a mutton bone and a beef bone.'

What about the stale bones?

Green says: 'Sometimes I have had one that was stale and stunk, and I eat it even then.'

Why?

'I eat it because I am hungered, I suppose,' says Green. 'You see we only have bread and gruel for breakfast and as there is no bread allowed on meat days we save our bread from breakfast, and then, having only gruel for breakfast we are hungry before dinner time. To satisfy our hunger a little, because a pint and a half of gruel is not much for a man's breakfast, we eat the stale and stinking meat.'

The men set to work, gathering up the dry bones and piling them into square boxes made of elm reinforced with metal brackets. In most cases they work in pairs, holding the box between them as they crush and pound its contents with a 28-pound ram made of iron and measuring more than a yard long. It takes quite some effort to lift the ram and bring it down to crack the bones, but some of the workers are perhaps not much older than ten. Over and again they bring the rams down, sending splinters flying up out of the box and occasionally into their faces. The men sweat and grimace, not least because of the smell. One man's hands are cracked and bleeding. Another's grime-stained face is patterned by tears of pain trickling down his cheeks.

Hour after hour the bones are crushed until they can be passed through a half-inch sieve. Each man is expected to produce a bushel and a half of dust a day, or around 80lbs. Farmers will pay perhaps 24 shillings for a ton of bone dust, a profit of 5 shillings a ton.

The workhouse is designed to be tough. The aim is to prevent the poorest people from starving to death by offering them food, shelter and medical care. It is not intended to offer a refuge for the idle. The workhouse should, it is argued, be 'the hardest taskmaster and the worse paymaster within the district' and should only give relief of a kind that 'none but the really destitute would accept'. The workhouse really is the last resort.

Andover Union, like many others across the country, was set up after Parliament passed the Poor Law Amendment Act in 1834. This new law was designed to crack down on the rising cost of relief paid out by parishes during an era of economic depression, poverty, working class protest and rising population and food prices. To save money, groups of thirty parishes are formed into a 'union'. Each Union has its own workhouse administered by the Poor Law Guardians. Then, rather than paying relief in cash to those who are struggling due to illness or unemployment, the Guardians decide whether to admit a person or their family to the workhouse. Such is the reputation of the workhouse that many potential paupers prefer to try their luck on the outside rather than give up their freedom. By all accounts the new, national system has been a success, with an estimated saving of £1 million, or around 20 per cent. And while the number of paupers has increased to more than 1.5 million out of a population of around 15 million, they are no longer cluttering the streets.

Opponents of the New Poor Law, however, object to the effective criminalisation of the destitute and unemployed. There are stories of husbands, wives and children being separated, their possessions confiscated, their bodies beaten and starved. But it took a fictional

124

character to arouse the most public sympathy. In 1837 Charles Dickens told the story of Oliver Twist, a young orphan boy who escaped his miserable existence in a workhouse only to take up with a gang of pickpockets.

Andover Union is in some ways worse than any workhouse conjured up by Dickens. The master here is Colin McDougal, a 52-year-old Scot who fought at Waterloo and reached the rank of Serjeant Major before being discharged in 1836 after his leg was crushed under a horse. Assisted by his wife as matron and his son as schoolmaster, McDougal runs the workhouse like a prison camp. At 6am the paupers are hauled from their beds ready for morning prayers, roll call and breakfast, which is usually six ounces of bread and 1.5 pints of gruel. One side of the dining room is for women and the other is for men. Talking is forbidden. At 7am they are set to work, whether in the bone yard or the kitchens or the classroom. Dinner varies – four days a week it is seven ounces of bread (six ounces for women and children) and two ounces of cheese. On Tuesday they have the luxury of eight ounces of cooked meat and half a pound of vegetables. Thursday there is 1.5 pints of soup. Saturday is five ounces of bacon (four ounces four women and children) and half a pound of vegetables. Then at 1pm the paupers return to work for another five hours. Supper is at 7pm, another six ounces of bread and 1.5 ounces of cheese. At 8pm it is time for bed. Lights are extinguished at 9pm and soon the day starts all over again.

The workhouse diet here at Andover is almost certainly the worst in the country, as it is less generous than even the most miserly diet suggested by the Poor Law Commission. So it is not surprising that the inmates are hungry enough to gnaw on bones or munch on raw potatoes dug up in the fields or thrown out for the chickens. As Aaron Astridge explains: 'I have seen the men clap raw potatoes into their mouths the same as you would an apple.' Elizabeth Gate, a 34-year-old mother-of-two agrees: 'I have seen children eat raw potatoes and the chicken food in the yard, potatoes and oats mixed together, and I have seen Mrs McDougal beat them for it.'

Other stories doing the rounds suggest that McDougal misbehaves worse than any inmate. He regularly gets drunk on duty and on one occasion was so intoxicated at dinner that he read the Lord's Prayer twice in succession. He canes any child who makes a mess or tries to run away. Remember Jimmy Brown in 1841, they say, who was thrashed so hard the cane broke across his back, just because he got an upset stomach and soiled his bed. Beatings of the children are common, says Jane Grace, who has been in the workhouse with her mother since the age of 11. 'I have been beaten a good many times. Mistress has beaten me, and master has beat us all right round the school. They would go round and fetch everyone a stripe on the head because we were making a noise.' Other punishments include being locked in a dark room for up to 10 hours at a time for refusing to eat the breakfast gruel.

Hannah Joyce tells us how she was humiliated by the McDougals after her one-month-old baby died only a few days after she entered the workhouse. 'It made a great noise with its breath. I put the child to the breast directly I got into bed. It sucked twice, and I took hold of the child under its armed and lifted it up on my arm. Twenty minutes later I found it struggling.' Hannah called for the matron but had to wait another 15 minutes for her to arrive. Mrs McDougal took one look at the infant and scolded Hannah: 'You good for nothing brute, you will be hanged for you have killed your child.' Mr McDougal joined in by calling her a whore and a faggot who should go to hell. Even when the inquest returned a verdict of death by natural causes (otherwise known as 'Visitation from God'), the McDougals ordered her to sleep with her child in the 'deadhouse' the night before burial. Hannah was then forced to carry the coffin through the centre of town to the churchyard a mile away. But that was not the end of it. When she finally left the workhouse a week later to go and live with her father in Chilbolton Mr McDougal organised a 'skimmington' to see her off. As Hannah explains: 'When I came down the steps a number of the women came round the corner with tin cups and spoon and plates and knives and firepans, rattling and hallooing. I saw Mr McDougal, he came down the steps laughing. I considered that I had not done anything to be punished for – I could not help the death of my child.'

THE WORKHOUSE

On top of that Mr McDougal sexually harasses many of the women employed in the workhouse as domestic servants. McDougal tried to kiss Ann Knight and Caroline Holt, the children's nurse Maria Laishley, and the pantry girl Sarah Cowdray. Mother-of-six Pricilla Weston, 36, tells us: 'He used to take liberties with me in the sick ward closet. He used to pull me in, unbutton his smallclothes then pulled up my clothes. I would not allow him to have connection with me. I resisted from him as well as I could.' When Priscilla ran away to avoid his attentions she was arrested, taken before the Magistrates and sentenced to three days in jail before being returned to the workhouse.

McDougal has no qualms about cheating on his wife, even though she once threatened to kill herself following one of their stormy arguments. Elizabeth Rout, a 52-year-old woman who has worked in the kitchens, the laundry and the sick ward, admits that she eventually accepted his proposals in return for food and drink. 'I considered myself, and I thought as the children were almost starved and he said he'd give me some victuals and some beer that if he asked me again I would. It took place up in the sick ward. He gave me some victuals and some beer.' She had sex with McDougal four or five times, including once in a room next to his wife's bedroom while her baby was asleep. Elizabeth confesses this matter-of-factly, which is perhaps not surprising given her extraordinary life so far. She was born into a pauper family in 1793 and at the age of 24 got hitched to a deserted soldier by the name of Hutchins. He soon deserted her too, and she took up with 'a very nice man' called Edward Winter. Five years later her husband returned and decided to sell her to Mr Winter at Andover Market for two shillings and sixpence. A year after that Mr Hutchins bought her back. In 1836, after their eldest son was hanged for arson for burning down a haystack in Salisbury, the family emigrated to America. Not long afterwards Mr Hutchins died and Elizabeth and her five children returned to England. Now, like her parents before her, she is dependent on the parish.

The list of complaints about the management of Andover workhouse is so long that some believe the poor are being deliberately treated harshly as a kind of revenge for the 'Swing Riots' that took place in the area in November 1830 in protest at low wages, lack of work and rising food prices. Mobs of angry and impoverished agricultural labourers armed with sledge hammers, sickles and axes burnt down haystacks and destroyed machinery to reinforce their demands for higher wages. Instead their wages continued to fall, to ten shillings per week. A total of ninety-nine rioters were sentenced to death but only two were hanged. The rest were shipped off to Australia.

If this theory is true, the Poor Law Guardians of Andover chose the right person to do it. Colin McDougal is no friend of the poor. In fact, it is claimed that every Saturday he gets drunk in the local inns and vows to his friends to murder every single pauper in the workhouse.

Rumours about the conditions in Andover Union led one of the Poor Law Guardians to write to his MP. The bone-crushing allegations were raised in the House of Commons in August 1845 but the Home Secretary replied that 'he could not believe such an abuse existed'. Further investigation confirmed the stories and a public inquiry was ordered in March 1846. The Select Committee reported that McDougal's conduct 'was marked by undue severity' and that he 'was utterly deficient in many of the qualities which are of essential importance – fairness and impartiality, a due sense of truth, a well-regulated temper and proper habits of self control.' Bone-crushing was effectively banned across the country and the Poor Law Commission was replaced by the Poor Law Board.

CHAPTER 20

Immigrants

*In which we visit Liverpool in 1850 following the
arrival of hundreds of thousands of Irish immigrants
fleeing the Great Famine*

They came in waves from across the sea. From Ireland, the land of hunger, famine and blight.

Every week more and more arrived by boat at the port of Liverpool. In January of 1847 there were five thousand a week. In February there were seven thousand a week. And in March the total hit ten thousand.

Ten thousand and twenty-nine men, women and children in the first week of March.

Ten thousand, six hundred and thirty men, women and children in the second week of March.

Eleven thousand, five hundred and twenty-two men, women and children in the third week of March.

Eleven thousand and forty-five men, women and children in the fourth week of March.

And still they kept coming.

Fifteen thousand, two hundred and ninety-one men, women and children in the first week of April.

Twelve thousand, eight hundred and fourteen in the second week.

Seventeen thousand, five hundred and seventeen in the third week.

Twelve thousand, three hundred and eighty-nine in the fourth week.

By the end of the year more than 260,000 passengers had travelled from Ireland to Liverpool. Who were they and why did they come? Almost all of them were Irish. Many passed through the bustling port on the way to a new life in America. Others sought their future in England; food, shelter, a decent job on the docks, or the railways, or the factories. Some, unable to work, turned to 'tramping' or applied for relief at the workhouse. But once they found themselves classed as paupers they faced being shipped back to Ireland at public expense under the settlement laws in force since the seventeenth century.

One of those at the 'Pass-House' awaiting removal is a woman who came to England in search of her errant husband. 'He left me no money,' she tells us. 'I pawned my clothes for four shillings and paid my passage to Liverpool. I thought I should find my husband there.' She followed his trail to Shrewsbury but he was nowhere to be found. Whether she stays here or returns to Ireland, she has nowhere to go but the workhouse.

Here too is a 14-year-old orphan named James, from County Down. He arrived in Liverpool after stowing away on a ship from Belfast. 'I covered myself over with hay, among the horses, when the captain came. The sailors soon found me out and one of them gave me a kick. I didn't care.' James stayed in Liverpool for half a day before setting out into the countryside. 'I had no money,' he tells us. 'I saw a boy in a cellar, eating his breakfast. He was an Irish boy and gave me half of his loaf and a drop of coffee. I begged on the road and a farmer one night gave me a good supper, a good bed and my breakfast.' James reached the market town of Ormskirk in Lancashire but fared no better there and ended up sleeping in the 'relieving office' before being sent back to Liverpool. He will now go back home to his aunt. 'I didn't like begging,' he confesses. 'I can't get a good bed by begging. I should like to work for a good bed and plenty of meat.'

Patrick came to Liverpool in the hope of finding a job on a farm. He paid a shilling for his passage across the sea but could not find any work and ended up being arrested for begging in Warrington. After spending two weeks in prison he ended up at a lodging house in Liverpool. And when his attempt at begging only earned him a single penny he decided to apply at the 'Pass House' to be returned to Ireland. 'When I get back to Ireland I shall have to go to the Union,' he admits.

According to the parish statistics, 15,020 Irish paupers were removed to Ireland during 1847, with another 581 to Scotland and twenty to the Isle of Man. The total cost was £4,633 in food, travel and a sixpence allowance. The following year just over 10,000 were removed at a cost of £2,600. This seems to be a pointless task – it is now estimated that there are 90,000 Irish in Liverpool, about a quarter of the population.

One 'scam' highlighted in a newspaper report is the practice of poor Irish women to come to Liverpool in the last month of their pregnancy so they can be given food, shelter and medical attention before, during and after giving birth. Once declared fit to be removed, they are returned to Ireland at public expense.

Liverpool is a wealthy town thanks to the docks bristling with ships carrying goods from the New World; cotton, grain and pork from America, rum and sugar from the West Indies and timber from Canada. Even so, it is struggling under the financial burden. The costs mount up: sending the Irish poor back home; operating the workhouse and refuges for the destitute; paying outdoor relief; tackling the spread of cholera and other diseases; policing the vagrants and beggars. There are also complaints that the new arrivals are happy to work for wages as low as sixpence a day. There are too many hands and not enough work.

One of the Irishmen eager for employment is 27-year-old John from Meath. He came to England ten years ago with savings of two shillings and sixpence. He found his first job in Manchester drawing sand from the river for 18 shillings a week. It was hard work, lasting 12 to 15 hours a day, but it kept him honest for five whole years. Now he thinks about it, he could have saved six shillings of that every week to saved up a total of £78. But when the work ran out he did not have anything to fall back on and had to go to the night asylum for his bed, six ounces of bread and a pint of coffee. 'I fell in with the tramps there and heard all their conversation about the different towns where they had been,' he explains. 'I got the first thoughts of tramping from them.' John tried tramping to Bolton but didn't like it much and was 'too proud to beg' on the road. But when he tried to look for work in Manchester and found nothing going, he set out for Stockport. 'I was all alone and not up to begging. I didn't like it. At that time I felt savage and would much sooner have robbed than begged.'

Eventually he had little choice but to start begging. In Macclesfield, still wearing his working dress, he got 'bits of bread and broken victuals'. He tramped to Shrewsbury but was put in jail for two weeks and forced to pick oakum. He tramped to Bridgnorth and Kidderminster and Gloucester. He returned to Manchester but nobody wanted to give him a job. 'Nothing went right with me,' he tells us. 'For two years after this I did not get above a fortnight's work at different times, though I was able and willing.'

James tramped to London and was spent three weeks in Tothill Fields Prison. With his hair cropped 'gaol bird' style, he had little chance of getting a job and returned to tramping. He tramped to Barnet and St Albans. He spent five months tramping his way to South Wales. 'I began to like tramping,' he admits. 'Some of the tramps are clever fellows, we have a good deal of fun at night. We tell stories. The best liar is the best man among the tramps. We sing songs, some of them very good songs, sentimental ones, some of them are very bad and some of them worse than bad. We always tell each other the best Unions to go to. I used to sleep in barns and always got a good breakfast in the morning, and very often a supper of cowal . . . it is made of cabbage, beef, taturs and all kinds of vegetables.' One image of the tramp he is keen to dismiss is that of the drunk. 'Tramps are not drunkards, they very seldom drink.'

In South Wales he finally struck lucky and got taken on as a navvy on the railway for 15 shillings a week for six months. After that he found work for another six months at a foundry at 12 shillings a week. He only lost the job when he refused to work for ten shillings a week and somebody else took it instead. 'I preferred work, however hard, to tramping,' he says, and insists he has never tried any of the vagrant tricks or 'lurks' such as posing as a broken-down parson or tradesman.

So in April 1849 he returned to London, staying in Unions along the way. He found no work there so headed north to Liverpool. There is no work here either, though a kindly clergyman gave him two shillings and sixpence.

132

IMMIGRANTS

What next?

James tells us: 'I hope this summer to get a chance somewhere or other. I would like to get out of England. I would go to America, or anywhere else where I could live. I shall leave Liverpool tomorrow and try my luck once more.'

In 1847 more than 109,000 people emigrated from the UK to Canada, another 142,000 to the United States, and nearly 5,000 to Australia and New Zealand. More than half left from Liverpool. The laws governing the removal of paupers to their 'place of settlement' remained in force until 1948. Paupers could not be removed if they had lived in a parish for five years (this was reduced to one year from 1865).

CHAPTER 21

Street Orphans

In which we speak to the flower girls and crossing-sweeper boys scraping a living on the streets of London in the middle of the nineteenth century

A young orphan girl with a dimpled chin sits on a bundle of rags clutching a bunch of wallflowers. She is perhaps 11 years old and looks as us with a mixture of suspicion, weariness and hope. Her mucky, bare feet poke out beneath the old, dark print frock and her shoulders and arms are wrapped in a shawl to keep out the breeze. A short distance away her older sister works the passing crowds of ladies and gentlemen, crying in sing-song 'A penny a bunch . . . wallflowers, violets, roses . . .' The older girl, even at 15 years of age, has the muddier complexion and pinched face of experience, although at least she has the luxury of wearing worn-out shoes. Soon she strikes gold – or at least copper – as a woman stops to remark: 'A penny my poor girl? Here's three half-pence for the bunch.'

The sisters are just two of the many children selling everything from fruits and nuts to small toys and firewood on the streets of London. One estimate puts the figure at somewhere around 10,000. It is difficult to know many of those are flower sellers but there is clearly a market for their brightly-coloured wares, as it is said that nearly a million bunches of cut flowers sold every year in the streets.

'I sell Primroses, when they're in, and Violets, and Wall-flowers and roses of different sorts, and pinks and carnations and mixed flowers and lilies of the valley and green lavender and mignonettte,' explains the older girl. 'The best sale of all is, I think, moss-roses. We do best of all on them.'

And who are their best customers?

'Gentlemen are our best customers,' she replies. 'I've heard that they buy flowers to give to the ladies. I think it's the sweetness as sells them. It's very little use offering any that's not sweet.'

The girls buy their flowers at Covent Garden market at one shilling for a dozen bunches. Their profit is made by splitting those twelve bunches up and turning them into eighteen slightly smaller bunches. On top of that another penny is spent on wrapping paper. Then they head out to St John's Wood or Hampstead or Highgate to find customers. 'The two of us doesn't make less than sixpence a day, unless it's very ill luck,' explains the girl. 'But religion teaches us that God will support us and if we make less we say nothing.'

They live with their 13-year-old brother – who works as a costermonger's boy – in a house of street sellers and labourers near Drury Lane. Although their room is large and has enough room for an old four-post bedstead, a table and a few chairs, one corner of it is taken up by an Irish married couple. A shred of privacy is provided by a curtain hung up between the two groups. The walls are rotten with damp and a single, flickering candle provides the only source of light at night. For this the three children pay two shillings a week, which leaves them with another two shillings a week to pay for food and living expenses.

'We live on bread and tea, and sometimes a fresh herring of a night,' says the older girl. 'Sometimes we don't eat a bit all day when we're out, sometimes we take a bit of bread with us, or buy a bit. My sister can't eat taturs [potatoes], they sicken her.'

The girl is proud that she has never 'troubled the parish' for relief money or food and that all three siblings can read, thanks to the charitable 'Ragged Schools' which offer free education in the poorest districts of the city. It is all the more surprising when you consider that both their mother and father died seven years ago.

For some girls flower-selling is the last resort before begging or prostitution (others might combine all three). One tells us that she used to live very comfortably until her father, a whitesmith, died of consumption. Her mother died last year after coming down with a cold.

135

She tells us: 'My mother used to fret dreadful as she lay ill about me, for she knew she was going to leave me. She used to plan how I was to do when she was gone. She made me promise to try and get a place and keep from the streets if I could, for she seemed to dread them so much. When she was gone I was left in the world without a friend.' Finding a job as a domestic servant proved impossible without a character reference and, after selling her furniture to survive, the girl ended up living at a lodging house and selling flowers on the streets to make a profit of sixpence a day. 'Of the sixpence I pay threepence for lodging, I get a half-pennyworth of tea, a half pennyworth of sugar. one pound of bread and a half-pennyworth of butter.'

'What I shall do in the winter I don't know,' she sobs. 'In the cold weather last year, when I could get no flowers, I was forced to live on my clothes, I have none left now but what I have on. What I shall do I don't know – I can't bear to think on it.'

* * *

Another profession seen as 'the last chance left of obtaining an honest crust' is that of crossing-sweeper. The sweepers, many of whom are elderly or disabled, offer a useful service to the pedestrian (particularly the ladies with their long trailing skirts) by clearing a path through the horse manure and other detritus littering the city streets. The only things you need to set up shop are a broom made out of branches and a claim to a position on the highway.

This useful service also offers the sweeper an excuse to beg money from passers-by. Here comes one now. 'Give a halfpenny to poor little Jack,' pleads the mucky-faced boy with large, mournful eyes. Jack is 15 years old and both his parents are dead. 'Father was a perfumer by trade and used to make hair dye and scent and pomatum,' the boy explains. 'He used to make a good deal of money but he lost it betting. I remember he used to come home tipsy and say he'd lost it on this or that horse, and then mother would coax him to bed and afterwards sit down and begin to cry.' Jack's mother sold up their furniture and brought him to London, where she earned a living making hairnets.

136

Jack stayed with his sister for a while until she got married and told him he had to leave and make his own way.

Jack says: 'So I bought a box and brushes and went cleaning boots and I done pretty well with them till my box was stolen from me by a boy.'

He has been sweeping crossings for two years now along with another five boys who claim the territory from St Martin's Church in Trafalgar Square to Pall Mall. 'I and another gets a crossing – those who gets on it first keeps it – and we stand on each side and take our chance. If I was to see two gentleman coming I should cry out "two toffs" and then they are mine, and my mate is bound not to follow them. If it's a lady and a gentleman we cries "a toff and a doll". If we both cry out together then we share.'

Jack makes most of his money when it is wet and yesterday earned three-and-a-half pence. 'We're always sure to make money if there's mud. I think we make fourpence every day. One day, the best I ever had, from nine in the morning till seven at night I made seven shillings and sixpence, and got not one bit of silver money among it.'

The only thing they have to watch out for is the police, as being caught with money on the streets can bring 14 days in prison for begging. Jack and his friends have developed a strategy for this: 'We never carries no pockets, for if the policemen find us we generally pass the money to our mates.' They also have a code word they use to alert each other to any constables approaching, as well as nicknames for each of them: Bull's Head, Bandy Shanks, and Old Cherry Legs.

At night the boys make more money by performing acrobatics, or 'tumbling' as they call it, for the enjoyment of gentlemen returning from the opera or the theatre. Jack says: 'When they've got a young lady on their arm they laugh at us tumbling; some will give us a penny, others threepence, sometimes a sixpence or a shilling, and sometimes a halfpenny. We either do the catun [Catherine] wheel or else we keep before the gentleman and lady, turning head over heels, putting our broom on the ground and then turning over it.'

One of the group, a ten-year-old boy called Johnny, is known as the 'King of the Tumblers' because of his acrobatic ability. 'I'm best at catenwheels,' he says. 'I can do 'em twelve or fourteen times running. When I gets up I feels quite giddy. I can tumble about forty times over head and heels. When I see anybody coming I say "please sir give me a halfpenny" and touches my hair and then I throw a caten wheel and I has a look at em and if I sees they are laughin' then I goes on and throw more of them. I think I can tumble the best of them.'

Then at 3am they all meet at the steps of St Martin's Church to count up their money before buying food, clothes or lodging at a house in for the night, unless it's warm and they can sleep outside. Jack tells us, 'We buys a pound of bread, twopence, and we gets haporth of tea and haporth of sugar. We make our own tea, they lends us a kettle, teapot and cups and saucers and all that. Once or twice a week we gets meat. We all club together and go into Newgate market and gets some pieces cheap and boils them at home. We tosses up who shall have the biggest bit and we divide the broth, a cupful in each basin until it's lasted out.'

Johnny, the King of the Tumblers, would be glad to get out of crossing-sweeping. 'I don't like it,' he tells us. 'In the winter we has to be out in the cold and in summer we have to sleep out all night or go asleep on the church steps regular tired out. Perhaps they've got the price of a lodging but they're hungry and they eat the money and then they must lay out. There's some of 'em will stop out in the wet for perhaps the sake of a halfpenny and get themselves sopping wet. I think all our chaps would like to get out of the work if they could.'

Abandoned and orphaned children – also known as 'Street Arabs' – continued to be a feature of London streets for the rest of the nineteenth century. In 1866 Thomas Barnardo set up the Barnardos charity to look after and educate destitute boys and girls in the East End. The National Society for the Prevention of Cruelty to Children was founded in 1884 (then under the name of the London Society for the Prevention of Cruelty to Children). Between 1870 and 1893 the Government passed a succession of laws which made attending school compulsory for all children aged between five and 13. By 1918 child 'vagrants' had virtually disappeared from the streets.

CHAPTER 22

The Casual Ward

*In which we visit a London workhouse in 1866 to experience
the sights and smells of the 'casual ward' occupied by
homeless tramps and vagrants*

Under the flickering gaslight wait the applicants for the casual ward
of a London workhouse. A family of four huddle together for warmth
against a noticeboard announcing rewards for missing children and
lost pets. The father holds his barefooted youngest daughter in his arms
while the mother, wrapped up in a striped bonnet and shawl, draws
two other girls in close. Next to them a small boy shivers in the frosty
air and an older man in a skewed top hat and scruffy coat and trousers
appears to nod off as he leans against the brick wall. Others slump
down on the floor, resting their weary legs after a day spent wandering
the streets. A mangy dog growls while a policeman examines its
owner's ticket of admission. Ahead of them a young mother, her ticket
approved, shuffles to the back of the queue clutching her baby to her
breast beneath a black shawl. Tagging along on her skirt-tails is her
eldest daughter, perhaps five years old, in a white bonnet, knee-length
skirt and baggy, wrinkled socks.

It is a scene that is repeated countless times every night across
London as the homeless poor, seeking to avoid a long-term stay in the
workhouse, take advantage of the casual wards established as a result
of the Metropolitan Houseless Poor Act of 1864. Opinions differ as to
the benefits of these 'free hostelries of the unemployed workpeople'.
Many believe that rather than assisting the temporarily distressed they
actively encourage a whole class of vagabonds to avoid hard work.
The journalist Henry Mayhew reckons there are more than 109,000

vagrants in England and Wales, including 13,500 in workhouses, 20,000 in various barns and tents and the rest in mendicant houses. Large numbers flock to the countryside in April or May before returning to London in December to take shelter during the winter. So while the casual ward prevents people from starving or dying of cold in the streets, they are also said to attract habitual beggars. To find out more, we will have to go undercover to investigate in turn the separate wards for men and for women and children.

MEN

We arrive at the men's ward in Lambeth workhouse with our body 'marked with every sign of squalor'. Our costume consists of a faded brown coat that is much too small to be considered anything but ill-fitting. It is held together at the front by a piece of twine rather than any buttons and the sleeves are much too short, having lost their cuffs. Our face is unwashed, unshaven and cast in shadow by the drooping brim of a battered 'billy-cock' hat. A cotton handkerchief knotted around our neck resembles a hangman's noose. Our hands are thrust despondently into our pockets for warmth. And to top off the look of a hardened tramp, our boots bear the scars of endless wandering in all weathers and across all terrains.

The porter answers our knock at the door with a short question: 'What do you want?'

'I want a lodging.'

The porter leads us into the hall and bids us to stand before a desk occupied by a clerk and a large ledger.

'You are late,' says the clerk.

'Am I, sir?'

'Yes. If you come in you'll have a bath, and you'll have to sleep in the shed.'

The clerk asks for our name, occupation and last place of residence and enters them into his book before directing the porter to give us a piece of bread and take us down a passage to the bathhouse. There are three large baths, each filled with dirty water the colour of mutton broth.

The bath attendant, known as the Tramp Major, tells us to take off all our clothes so that they are not stolen by the other casuals. 'Tie 'em up in your hank'sher, and I'll lock 'em up till the morning', he adds, handing us a blue striped shirt, a rug and a ticket to reclaim our bundle of clothes. The Tramp Major then leads us across cold flagstones to the room in which we are to spend the night.

In fact the room is more of a shed. There are three whitewashed walls (or dirtwashed in this case) enclosing a space roughly 30ft square. Entrance is effected through a wide door consisting of a crudely hung canvas that does not even attempt to isolate its occupants from the cold. Still, at least the gusts of freezing air combat the overwhelming smell of damp. A single gaslight jutting out from one wall provides the sole illumination besides the moon. What looks like an earthen floor is in fact stone encrusted with filth. But most of the space is taken up by two rows of men and boys lying side-by side on mattresses stuffed with hay. There are perhaps thrity of them all together. Some lie so still enveloped in their rugs that they look more like corpses laid out after a particularly devastating railway accident. Others squat upon their beds smoking tobacco, singing ribald ditties or exchanging obscene jokes.

'I like to be a swell, a-roaming down Pall-mall, Or anywhere,—I don't much care, so I can be a swell.'

Nobody pays us much attention as we shuffle inside. One man, naked to the waist, asks us to pass us a tin pot of water: 'Old pal, hand me a swig, I'm werry night garspin'. He advises us to choose a bunk on the left side of the shed out of the wind. However the straw bag we select has a large bloodstain in the middle. We turn it over to expose the cleaner side and lie down under our rug before beginning to munch on our bread. Meanwhile the other casuals debate over the best and worst workhouses in London. For the worst they settle on Tottenham and Poplar, where casuals sleep on bare boards rather than beds.

At half-past nine in the evening we close our eyes to prepare for sleep only to be disturbed by a flurry of oaths from a young man lying with two of his friends on a single bed nearby. All three then turn to smoking, swapping anecdotes and spitting on the floor. Three or four others in the shed then speak up to demand they shut up or face the consequences. We are soon caught in the middle of a fearsome row as each side issues taunts and threats and invites the other to fight 'a round'.

Just as we are beginning to despair of getting any sleep a teenage boy arrives, perhaps 15 years old with large blue eyes and short hair. He clutches a cap beneath his arm.

'What yer got in yer cap, Kay?' calls out a voice.

'Who'll give me part of his doss?' asks the youth. 'My eyes and limbs if I ain't perishin! Who'll let me turn in with him for half my toke?'

We gather from this he is offering half his bread ration in return for a share of a warm bed. Soon enough he is snuggled up with the three men sleeping next to us.

'You was too late for skilly, Kay. There's skilly now, nights as well as mornins,' one of the men tells the youth.

'Don't you tell no bleeding lies,' Kay answered, incredulously.

'Blind me, it's true!'

'Well, I don't want no skilly, leastways not to-night,' replies Kay. 'I've had some rum. Two glasses of it, and a blow out of puddin' – regler Christmas plum puddin'. Kay then opened his cap to reveal two slices of bread and butter. 'There, share em amongst yer, and somebody give us a whiff of bacca.'

Kay next proposes a game of 'Swearing Club', the rules of which state that anyone who swears in the course of conversation receives a punch. Unless that is, the oath appears in the Bible. Anyone who seeks to deliver a punch for an oath from the Bible will himself receive a double punching. Some of the group appear so taken with the sport that they deliberately slip up, or attempt to outdo each other in profanity.

At last the church bells toll midnight and the other casuals fall quiet and attempt to get some sleep. The only sounds to be heard are the flapping of the canvas curtain, assorted snoring and coughing, or the fierce scratching of fingers upon itchy skin.

Still sleep comes far too slowly.

Then at one o'clock there is a banging on the porter's door as another ten men turn up looking for beds. They tramp into the shed, grabbing any spare hay mattress they can find or flinging themselves next to anyone who has one to himself.

Finally at half-past two, when the Major comes to count us, everybody is quiet. But we still cannot sleep. We monitor the church bells as time passes at a snail's pace. At six o'clock the factory bells call the working man to labour but nobody in the shed moves a muscle. Finally at seven, the workhouse clock goes 'Clang!'

'Now, then! wake em up!', cries the Tramp Major. We sit up, eager to collect our belongings and be gone.

Nobody else stirs, though some curse the bell.

Two paupers from the workhouse call out the ticket numbers. Thirty two. Twenty eight. Fifteen. Eventually our number is called and we hand over our shirt and ticket to collect our ragged bundle of clothing and shoes.

We exit the shed and join the crowd around a pail of water and soap in the yard. Then, after washing our face, and a good deal of hanging around, it is time for breakfast. A baker's man arrives with a huge wooden tray piled up with slices of bread. There is one slice each although it is all too quickly devoured by the hungry casuals. A cry of 'Skilly, skilly!' starts up. Insults are hurled, and oaths sworn, before a loud 'hooray!' erupts when two steaming pails arrive. Each of us receive a yellow basin to receive approximately three-quarters of a pint of gruel. The others lap it up, though it is in fact nothing more than a mixture of oatmeal and water with not a hint of salt or other flavouring. Still, at least it is hot enough to warm our hands as well as our stomachs.

There is now only one thing between us and the exit – a dose of hard labour. We are taken back to the shed and instructed to turn iron cranks protruding from the wall. Doing so will set a flour mill grinding on the other side of the wall. Our task is to grind four bushels of corn yet nobody seems in a hurry to complete the task. No sooner has the taskmaster left the shed than the casuals take their hands off the crank and set to smoking, mending their clothes or cutting each other's hair.

Others play practical jokes, dipping a rag in grease from the crank axles and smearing it over a man's face. Only when the taskmaster returns to the shed to they suddenly rise up and spin their cranks round at a furious rate, as they bellow out their song.

> We'll hang up the miller on a sour apple tree,
> We'll hang up the miller on a sour apple tree,
> We'll hang up the miller on a sour apple tree,
> And then go grinding on.
> Glory, glory, Hallelujah . . .

By the time the bell rings out to signify the grinding of the fourth bushel it is already eleven o'clock. With that the yard gate is opened and we are free to leave. Glory, glory Hallelujah.

WOMEN

Our disguise as a 'female casual' consists of an old dirty blue velvet bonnet, a torn grey skirt, a checkcloth shawl and worn-out boots. And, of course, plenty of dirt to convince the officials of our distress. Gaining entry to the workhouse is not straightforward. First we have to obtain an order of admission from Lambeth police station by undergoing a kind of interrogation by the inspector on duty.

'What do you want?'

'What is your name?'

'Your age?'

'Where did you sleep last?'

'What are you?'

We explain that we are a hawker of embroidery but have neither stock nor money to buy stock. The inspector eyes us suspiciously but appears to be satisfied by the decrepit state of our boots.

'Here is your order, go along', he says.

It is 9pm by the time we reach the door of the workhouse. The porter lets us in and hands us over to a stout woman around 50 years old. 'Come along, this way to the bath,' she says, leading us to a room with three zinc baths filed with hot and cold water. There is soap, a clean towel and a blue gown to wear once our clothes are taken away.

Then it is off to the sleeping ward. It is a long room filled with twenty-four wooden troughs laid side by side. Each trough is about a foot high and contains a straw bed and a thick rug. Eight of the troughs are already occupied by other women, all of whom appear to be engaged in picking things from their bodies and their clothes. It is only when we get closer that we realise the whole place is crawling with lice and other vermin.

One of the woman notices us looking on in horror and tells us: 'You will not be clean for long, for the beds in these places are all infected.'

Another lady picks bugs from her body one by one and cracks them between her nails. She says, 'I don't care how many lice I have but I can't abide them Pharaoh flights [fleas].'

'Ah we have more peace in winter, there are fewer vermin,' says a third.

The abundance of bugs means that everybody is almost constantly scratching themselves as they compare the relative merits of different casual wards across London. One woman nicknamed 'Cranky Sal' claims that Richmond and Marylebone have feather beds. Newington has no washing facilities and at Whitechapel the vermin run in and out of the cracks in the whitewashed walls 'like bees at the entrance to a hive'. Perhaps the worst is at St George's in the East near the docks, where the ward is an underground cellar connected to a water closet that stinks of death. 'So help me God I will never go there again, I would rather go to prison a hundred times.'

One of the complaints about Lambeth is the length of time you are kept at work 'picking oakum', the unravelling and taking apart of old, tarry ropes.

'Ah if it wasn't for that I would come here every night,' says one woman, 'but I do not care while the weather is fine, I would as live sleep out of doors as in.'

Another concludes: 'I would be damned if I would ever pay for a night's lodging even if I had a pound in my pocket.'

Cranky Sal is an interesting character who has been known to trade on her name to get a place in the 'imbecile ward', where you eat meat every day and do not have to work. Sal is perhaps 37 years old but one side of her face has been affected by a stroke or fit. She tells us: 'I beg and pick up what I can, and go about anywhere for a bit of food or a night's lodging. Sometimes I make do on what they give 'em at these places here. Sometimes I get a few pence given me. For months I have not tasted meat until last Saturday, when I met a crippled old woman who gave me a piece of bread and meat and three quarters of a pint of beer. I am very badly off now. I have applied several times for an order to go into the workhouse but they refused to give me one whilst the weather is fine. I mean to go and ask the guardians for five shillings and if they give it to me I want to buy a clean gown, a pair of shoes and a few pipelights to sell. I am so dirty now that I do not know what to do. And I want some soap to wash me and my clothes more than food.'

More women enter during the night, including one who has been picking roses for one penny per bushel. 'Strike me dead if it is not too bad, for I only earned fivepence all the day,' she grumbles. 'Last year it was much better and I got twopence a bushel.'

The night passes slowly to a soundtrack of scratching. It is only when dawn arrives that the vermin appear to let up. Yet, no sooner do we manage to snatch a little sleep than the bell rings and it is time to get up.

Following a breakfast of skilly and bread – during which many of the women continue to pick vermin from their clothes – the oakum is brought in for picking. Everyone is given a pound of old, hard rope. It is tough labour that leaves your hands aching and sore. Four of the women try for a while and then refuse to do any more. We ask them, 'Why don't you get on? You will never be let out today.'

'Oh no, they cannot keep you in after twelve o'clock,' they reply. 'We don't hurt ourselves with work . . . such places as this ought to be set fire to.'

After an hour of work one woman suddenly jumps up in a frantic state, crying out: 'I cannot bear it!' At first we think she means the oakum, but it quickly becomes clear she is referring to the constant itching. In a frenzy she strips herself down to her bonnet and shawl and tears her clothes to rags.

The supervisor arrives shortly to demand: 'What have you done that for? You ought to be ashamed of yourself.'

'I could not bear it any longer and I cannot help it,' the woman replies. She is eventually provided with an old petticoat, a checked chemise and a jacket of workhouse cotton.

At eleven o'clock the oakum is taken away from everybody, whether finished or not, and we are allowed to leave. We exit the workhouse looking even more dishevelled than we did on entering.

The number of casual ward beds at London Unions doubled between 1863 and 1866 to more than 2,000, at a time when the city's tramp population was estimated at 12,000. The year 1867 saw the establishment of the Metropolitan Asylums Board (MAB) and the construction of several new casual wards, including one at the Marylebone Workhouse which boasted hot baths, clean and disinfected clothes, mattresses stuffed with coconut husk, flock pillows, and a supper consisting of six ounces of bread and a pint of gruel. 'A board of Good Samaritans could do no more,' raved one reviewer. The MAB was given responsibility for the care of London's sick poor at workhouse infirmaries and the treatment of non-pauper patients at free fever hospitals. From these humble beginnings emerged the National Health Service in 1948.

CHAPTER 23

Sleeping Rough

*In which we go among the homeless and unemployed men
and women sleeping rough in London in the late 1880s*

The midday scene at St James' Park has become a familiar one in 1887, the year of Queen Victoria's Golden Jubilee. At a time when the British Empire is hailed as the greatest the world has ever seen, the homeless dot the expanse of green grass like so many molehills. Some are sleeping, while others gaze disinterestedly at the horizon or up into space. A dog licks at the hand of one man dozing under the shadow of his cap while a few feet away a woman curls up under a flimsy blanket.

It is hard not to notice the homeless problem in the centre of the so-called 'modern Babylon'. As well as St James' Park, the poor gather under Waterloo Bridge, in Covent Garden Market or in shop doorways, goods yards and other nooks and corners that offer shelter from the elements. One of the most popular places is along the Embankment between Blackfriars and Westminster. Here scores of men – a total of 368 were counted on one particular night – huddle together on benches or the stone abutments that offer some protection from the wind.

'You see there's nowhere else so comfortable,' explains an elderly man who used to work on the London omnibuses before coming down with bronchitis. 'I was here four nights this week. I had no money for lodgings, couldn't earn any, try as I might. I've had one bit of bread to-day nothing else whatever, and I've earned nothing to-day or yesterday; I had threepence the day before. Gets my living by carrying parcels, or minding horses, or odd jobs of that sort. You see I haven't got my health, that's where it is. What's the good of a man what's got bronchitis and just left the infirmary? Who'll engage him, I'd like to know? Besides, it makes me short of breath at times, and I can't do much.' The man tells us his wife died years ago and his son is away on a ship somewhere. Besides, most nights the weather is fair and a bit of waste paper takes the hardness out of the seats. 'We have women sleep here often, and children, too. They're very well conducted, and there's seldom many rows here, you see, because everybody's tired out. We're too sleepy to make a row.'

Others here include a 54-year-old confectioner from Dartford who lost his job because of his rheumatism, unemployed labourers, tailors, sawyers, distillers and drivers, and a former banker who is now too ill and old to get another job. The latter points at the greasy rags hanging from his body and tells us: 'I have a brother-in-law on the Stock Exchange, but he won't own me. Look at my clothes. Is it likely?' A 16-year-old boy explains he has earned 1½-pence profit today doing odd jobs and selling matches but has slept on the Embankment every night for a month. But how did he end up on the streets in the first place? It probably goes back to when he was sent away to Feltham Industrial School for playing truant. He says that when he returned home from Feltham his mother chucked him out because he couldn't give her any money to pay for drink.

Yet more walk the streets until the early morning when they can try getting a job early in the morning to earn a few coppers for food. One man tells us: 'I've been walking the streets almost day and night these two weeks and can't get work. I've got the strength, though I shan't have it long at this rate. I only want a job. This is the third night running that I've walked the streets all night; the only money I get is by minding blacking-boys' boxes while they go into Lockhart's for their dinner. I got a penny yesterday at it, and twopence for carrying a parcel, and to-day I've had a penny. Bought a ha'porth of bread and a ha'penny mug of tea.'

The lack of work might be blamed on the severe economic depression of 1885/6. But some claim that the numbers of rough sleepers in London soared after the much-publicised Mansion House appeal which raised £80,000 following riots by the unemployed and homeless in the West End in February 1886. People flocked to the city to receive handouts from the organisers who hoped that their generosity would prevent any further threat to the property of the respectable property owners. The money soon ran out but large numbers continue to sleep rough, most noticeably in Trafalgar Square.

The Square has become the meeting place of both the unemployed and casual workers as well as the ideal spot for political meetings to convert the masses to their cause. Today one crowd are waiting for one such meeting on the steps of St Martin's Church while other groups of 'ragged and haggard men' talk among themselves.

'Hullo, Bill, wot 'ev yer had for breakfast?'

'Nowt; wot did you get?'

'Arf a pound o' dry rooty [bread]; cadged it.'

Another woman starts up about a political meeting in Clerkenwell Green. 'Coppers didn't dare to interfere and very soon we shall have the beggars down – them and the rich folks as are enjoyin' themselves while we're a-starving.'

'That's the talk, mother,' replies one of the men.

Every group in the Square appears to share the same dislike of the rich and resentment at the condition of the poor. Their feelings are mirrored by the speeches given by socialist and Irish agitators. 'We are slaves,' cries one. 'Years ago Parliament spent millions of money to set free the black slaves; but now-a-days we have what is worse, we have white slaves, and Parliament will let them go on slaving till they die and will not stir a step or move a finger to help these!'

Once the speeches have finished a procession sets off towards Westminster Abbey behind the red flag of socialism. The young journalist Howard Goldsmid reckons the group amounts to a few thousand but is not one of those who view them as an unruly mob prone to violence. 'They say hard things of their betters: but they are hungering in a land of plenty. They threaten violence: but their wives and little ones are starving, and perhaps homeless. They have borne much. Year after year they have tasted, many of them, Winter's want and woe, and their pleading has elicited a sneer, while at least it would seem that their threats have evoked an answer. Don't blame them too severely, don't criticise them too harshly. They are men with the wants and cravings of men, but they have also the higher and nobler characteristics of mankind, and it is the duty of society to bring them out and utilise them.'

As night falls the police are acting on orders to 'move on' anyone trying to spend the night at the Square and issue them with a ticket to stay at a casual ward, refuge or lodging house. The homeless, on the other hand, insist that the casual wards are all full and hundreds are being turned away. Here is an officer addressing a small group of men on one of the terraces. 'Now you really must move on. We've strict orders to keep this place clear. You must move on. Get to the casual ward, why don't you.' If any of the group lingers too long, the officer gives them a gentle push.

One of the men refuses to move. He claims to be an out-of-work painter and glazier. He spent a month sleeping on the Embankment but moved here to get out of the cold. Told to go to a casual ward, he replies: 'I am a British working man and I won't go to any such place.' He also refuses to touch the workhouse, it being 'nothing more than a public human slaughter-house'.

'Then if you won't clear off the Square and you won't go to the casual ward, I must lock you up,' replies a police inspector.

'Very well,' says the man. 'Thank God I shall have a roof over my head tonight anyhow.' He will be brought up before the Magistrate the next morning but the prospect of further time in jail seems not to bother him very much.

Another fellow tells a policeman that the casual ward in Drury Lane is full. 'Can't help that,' replies the officer. 'You can't stay here. I've got strict orders against it, and if you can't get in one casual ward you must go to another.' He is told to go to a casual ward in Buckingham Palace Road instead, but that one has been full since four o'clock in the afternoon.

Eventually a kind officer issues us with a ticket. It reads:

151

Please give the bearer one night's lodging for this ticket and charge the amount to John James Jones.
No 6613

Director of the London Samaritan Society and Homerton Mission

This Ticket will entitle the bearer to a night's lodging if taken to either of the Lodging Houses named on the other side of this card.

On the back are the addresses of fourteen lodging houses in the area of Westminster and the Strand. We are told that each of these places claims to be 'full up for them tickets', whether because they really are full or they prefer to hold out for paying customers. The only thing left to do is to tramp around the city or seek out a gateway or doorstep away from patrolling police officers. After much wandering we find some unattended steps leading from Farringdon Road to Holborn Viaduct. But no sooner have our eyes closed than a police officer swings his 'bull's eye' lantern on our face. 'What are you doing there? Be off now and look sharp about it. Go to the casual ward or somewhere.'

Dejectedly we slope off once more into the night in search of rest.

On 13 November 1887 the 'Bloody Sunday' riot broke out in Trafalgar Square after police and troops moved in during a demonstration by at least 10,000 people. The next decade saw the growth of the trade union movement and in 1900 the Labour Party was founded. Hundreds continued to sleep rough in London throughout the 1890s and early twentieth century.

Epilogue

The Victorian preoccupation with poverty continued into the twentieth century. Writers and journalists revisited the subject over and over again, from Jack London in *People of the Abyss* (1903) and Mary Higgs in *A Tramp Among Tramps* (1904) to George Orwell in *Down and Out in Paris and London* (1933), while the researcher Seebohm Rowntree conducted surveys of the poor in York in 1899, 1935 and 1951.

During the same period the Old Age Pension and National Insurance were introduced (1908–11) and paupers were given the vote along with all men over 21 and women over 30 (1918). The word 'pauper' itself was officially retired when the workhouses were remodelled as 'Public Assistance Institutions' under the control of local authorities in 1929. By then their residents were mostly the elderly, sick and infirm.

In 1942 the Beveridge Report, which paved the way for the modern Welfare State, identified five 'social evils' that have featured heavily in this book: squalor, ignorance, want, idleness and disease. In 1948 the old Poor Law was replaced with the National Health Service and benefits for the homeless, unemployed, disabled and sick, single mothers, widows and families. But none of them would consider themselves as paupers.

So what next? In the twenty-first century the old image of the 'sturdy beggar' has been replaced with that of the benefit scrounger. Both are said to choose idleness over hard work and take advantage of the generosity of others. And while England has come a long way since the sixteenth century, we continue to debate the same social issues. It may be that after 60 years of the Welfare State the pendulum is swinging back the other way. But how should the benefits system be reformed (or replaced)? And if it is, do we risk rediscovering the problems of the past?

Notes and Sources

1. Domesday

The description of the slave ritual is taken from *Leges Henrici Primi* (c.1200), edited by L. J. Downer (1972). The journey from Winchester to Gloucester is based on actual entries in the Domesday Book for Hampshire, Wiltshire and Gloucestershire. The 'interview' with the ploughman in the fields is taken from *Aelfric's Colloquy*, an imaginary dialogue for monastic school pupils at Cerne Abbas between 989 and 1002. Details of the state of England at this time are drawn from the Anglo-Saxon Chronicle, the Ecclesiastical History of Ordericus Vitalis and the chronicle of Henry Huntingdon. See also *The Domesday Quest* by Michael Wood (1986), *The Making of the Domesday Book* by V. H. Galbraith (1961), *Domesday Book*, edited by Elizabeth Hallam and David Bates (2000), *The Normans* by David Crouch (2002), *Anglo-Norman England* by Marjorie Chibnall (1986), *Dress in Anglo-Saxon England*, by Gale Owen-Crocker (1986) and *The Winchester Story* by Barry Shurlock (1986).

2. The King of the Poor

The story of William FitzOsbert can be found in the chronicles of William of Newborough, Roger of Hovedon, Ralph Diceto and Gervase of Canterbury. The speech of Longbeard is given by William of Newborough. See also 'The Bearded Revolutionary', an essay by G. W. S. Barrow in *History Today* (October 1969). The contrasting descriptions of London in the late twelfth century are adapted from William FitzStephen's introduction to his biography of Thomas à Becket and the Chronicle of Nicholas of Devizes.

3. Mendicants

The description of the conditions in which the Franciscans lived when they first came to England is adapted from *The Friars and how they came to England* by Thomas of Eccleston (translated by Father Cuthbert, 1903). Any quotations are taken from this work or the writings of Francis himself. See also *St Francis of Assisi* by Father Cuthbert (1933) and *The Cambridge Companion to St Francis of Assisi*, edited by Michael Robson (2012). The Franciscan rules are taken from the 1221 'Rule of the Continent Brothers and Sisters'.

4. Black Death
The scene in the abandoned plague village is based on a number of descriptions of conditions at the time by chroniclers and other witnesses, including Boccaccio in Italy. Other details, such as the inscription on the church wall, come from sources contained in modern works such as *The Black Death* by George Deaux (1969), *Black Death: The Complete History* by Ole Benedictow (2004), *Black Death* by Philip Ziegler (1969), *A History of Bubonic Plague in the British Isles* by J. F. D. Shrewsbury (1970), *The Black Death in England* edited by W. M. Ormrod and P. G. Lindley (1996), and *Daily Life during the Black Death*, by Joseph P Byrne (2006). The Great Famine of 1315 is described in the *Vita Edwardi Secundi*. Details about Leicester come from the chronicle of Henry Knighton covering the period 1337 to 1396. Full texts of The Ordinance of Labourers and the Statute of Labourers are available online.

5. Rebellion
The narrative of events during the Peasants' Revolt is based on accounts contained in the chronicles of Froissart, Henry Knighton, Thomas Walsingham, the *Anonimalle*, Higden's *Polychronicon* and *Eulogiam Historiarum*. Their accounts vary as to dates and events, and Froissart's account already reads like a fictionalised version of events. For more on John Ball and his letters see Brian Bird, *Rebel before his time, a study of John Ball and the English Peasants' Revolt of 1381* (1987). See also *The Peasants' Revolt of 1381*, edited by R. B. Dobson (1970), and *Summer of Blood* by Dan Jones (2009). For an overview of fourteenth-century life see *The Time Traveller's Guide to Medieval England* by John Mortimer (2008).

6. To the Spital House

The dialogue with the porter and the beggar at the spital house gate is adapted from Robert Copland, *The Hye Way to the Spyttell Hous* (c. 1529–34). His account was based on a spital house in London (probably St Bart's) – the action has been moved to York for the purposes of this chapter. Information on St Leonard's Hospital from P. H. Cullum, *Cremetts and Corrodies* (1991). Details of York are taken from *Leland's Itinerary in England and Wales* (1535–7), and R. K. Booth's *York* (1990).

7. The Counterfeit Crank

The meeting with Nicolas Gennings and the description of types of beggar are adapted from Thomas Harman, *A Caveat or Warning for Common Cursetors, Vulgarly called Vagabonds* (c.1566). See also *The Fraternity of Vagabonds*, imprinted by John Aederley (c.1563–71) and William Harrison's *Description of England* (1577). For more on the treatment of beggars in the sixteenth century, see C. J. Ribton-Turner, *A History of Vagrants and Vagrancy, and Beggars and Begging* (1887), Anne M. Scott (ed.), *Experiences of Poverty in Late Medieval and Early Modern England and France* (2012), William C. Carroll, *Fat King, Lean Beggar* (1996), and A. L. Beier, *Masterless Men* (1985).

8. A Census of the Poor

The meeting with Edmonde Abbott is adapted from a 1561 court record included in William Hudson, *Selected Records of the City of Norwich* (1910), vol. 2, p. 180. Details of the census adapted from J. F. Pound, The Norwich Census of the Poor (1971) (the census can also be found online at http://www.welbank.net/norwich/1570/). See also J. F. Pound, *Tudor and Stuart Norwich* (1988) and E. M. Leonard, *The Early History of English Poor Relief* (1900), which includes the story of Benet Gedwyis. Details of St Paul's and St Giles' Hospitals from William Page (ed.), *A History of the County of Norfolk, vol. 2 (1906)*.

9. Bridewell

Details of Bridewell from Edward O'Donoghue, *Bridewell Hospital*

(1923) and William G. Hinkle, *A History of Bridewell Prison* (2006). Hinkle also contains the definition of 'thriftless poor' used by the Select Committee in 1552/3, and extracts of the experiences of particular inmates, including Richard Fullwood's stinking cell in 1594, Thomas Doulton's eight months of hemp beating in 1591, and Thomas Ellwood's entrance to Bridewell in 1662. For the background on poverty and poor relief in England at this time see E. M. Leonard, *The Early History of English Poor Relief* (1900) and A. L. Beier, 'Social Problems in Elizabethan London', *Journal of Interdisciplinary History*, 9(2) (1978). The dialogue with the inmates of Bridewell is adapted from a visit recounted by Ned Ward in *The London Spy* of c. 1699. The text of the 1601 Act for the Relief of the Poor is freely available online.

10. Witch Hunt

For more details about the mysterious life of Matthew Hopkins see Richard Deacon, *Witchfinder General* (1976). Accounts of the trials of Elizabeth Clarke and others at Chelmsford in 1645 can be found online at http://www.witchtrials.co.uk (including a section from the diary of Nehemiah Wallington). The number of witches on trial varies from twenty-three to thirty, depending on the source, as do the names of the witches and the number that were hanged. The interview with Hopkins is adapted from Hopkins' own leaflet *The Discovery of Witches* (1647). See also John Stearne's own pamphlet *Discovery of Witches* (c. 1648).

Civil War details come from *The Autobiography of Joseph Lister* (1821); Tristram Hunt, *The English Civil War at First Hand* (2002); Diane Purkiss, *The English Civil War, a People's History* (2006); John Adair, *By The Sword Divided* (1983); Martyn Bennett, *The Civil Wars Experienced* (2000); John Morrill (ed.), *Reactions to the English Civil War* (1983); Robert Morris, *The Sieges of Taunton* (1995); G. E. Aylmer (ed.), *The Levellers in the English Revolution*; Rice Bush, *The Poor Man's Friend* (1649); and *The Memoirs of Ann, Lady Fanshaw*, edited by John Loftis (1979).

11. At the Fair
Details about the fair including the traders' calls, the exhibitions and the monstrosities are adapted from Henry Morley, *Memoirs of Bartholomew Fair* (1859), which includes excerpts from Ben Johnson's play *Bartholomew Fayre*. The story about the Queen disguising herself to go to a fair (in Audley End) relates to 1670 and can be found in a letter in the manuscripts of Sir Henry Ingilby in *The Royal Commission on Historical Manuscripts*, 6th report (1877), p. 367. Further details of London at this time come from Liza Picard, *Restoration London* (1997). Some of the 'freak show' exhibits relate to the later years of the seventeenth century but have been added for colour. For the list of prostitutes see the pamphlet 'A catalogue of jilts, cracks, prostitutes, night walkers, whores, she-friends, kind women and others of the Linen-lifting tribe, who are to be seen every night in the cloisters in Smithfield, from the hours of Eight to eleven during the time of the fair', dated 28 August 1691.

12. Bedlam
The conversations with the inmates in Bedlam are adapted from Ned Ward's account in *The London Spy* of 1699 and the pamphlet *A Description of Bedlam with an account of its present inhabitants, both male and female*, printed for T. Payne in 1722. Historical detail on Bedlam is taken from Paul Chambers, *Bedlam* (2009).

13. The Common Side
Details of the conditions in the Marshalsea c. 1729 are taken from *A Report from the Committee Appointed to Enquire into the State of the Gaols of this Kingdom; The Miseries of Gaols and the Cruelty of Gaolers*; reports of the trials of William Acton on four charges of murder in *Cobbett's Complete Collection of State Trials* (1819); and *A Journal of My Life inside the Marshalsea* by John Baptist Grano (1729). See also the essay by Jerry White, 'Pain and Degradation in Georgian London', *History Workshop*, 68(1) (2009).

14. Gin

The hidden Gin shop scene is adapted from *The Life and Uncommon Adventures of Captain Dudley Bradstreet* (1760). The lifestyle of the Clay family is taken from the Proceedings of the Old Bailey, case t17380412-56. The young girl, Eleanor Clay, died from an infection. The lodger was accused of raping the child but was acquitted. The account of the Gin sellers on the route to Tyburn is taken from *A Trip from St James to the Royal Exchange*, by Edward Withers (1744). Other details of the 'Gin Craze', including the story of Judith Defour and the spontaneously combusting Gin drinkers, taken from Jessica Warner, *Craze: Gin and Debauchery in an Age of Reason* (2003), and Patrick Dillon, *Gin: The Much Lamented Death of Madam Geneva* (2004).

15. Foundlings

Details of the 117 infants received on the first day of 'general reception' come from the hospital records kept at the London Metropolitan Archives (billet books, admission registers and apprenticeship registers). See also R. H. Nichols and F. A. Wray, *The History of the Foundling Hospital* (1935); Gillian Pugh, *London's Forgotten Children* (2007); and Ruth McClure, *Coram's Children* (1981). The description of the scene outside the hospital comes from the *British Spy* newspaper of 12 June 1756.

16. Night Walkers

Details of events at St Martin's Roundhouse are taken from the reports of both trials of William Bird on the *Proceedings of the Old Bailey Online* website. See also the essay by Tim Hitchcock on the subject in Tim Hitchcock and Heather Shore (eds), *The Streets of London* (2003). Details of the twenty-five girls brought before Sir John Fielding come from Fielding's *A Plan of the Asylum or House of Refuge for Orphans and other Deserted Girls*, cited by Francis Place (British Library, Add. MSS, 27825). See also Fielding's *A Plan for the Preservatory and Reformatory for the benefit of deserted girls and penitent prostitutes* (1758). The episode involving James Boswell is taken from his

London Journal of 1763. Background details on prostitution in Georgian London, including Harris' List, are drawn from Hallie Rubenhold, *The Covent Garden Ladies* (2005); Tony Henderson, *Disorderly Women* (1999); Dan Cruickshank, *The Secret History of Georgian London; Low Life, or one half of the world knows not how the other half live* (1750); and *The Memoirs of Fanny Murray* (1759).

17. The Black Poor
The descriptions of Billy Waters, Joseph Johnson, Toby and Charles McGee come from John Thomas Smith, *Vagabondiana* (1815), and James Walvin and P. Edwards, *Black Personalities in the Era of the Slave Trade* (1983). For more information on slavery, the Black Poor and the Sierra Leone settlement see Simon Schama, *Rough Crossings* (2006), Stephen Braidwood, *Black Poor and White Philanthropists* (1994) and Folarin Shyllon, *Black People in Britain* (1977).

18. Poor Stockingers
The words of the frame-workers come from the *Report of the Select Committee on Petitions of Framework Knitters* (1812) and the *Report of the Select Committee on the Framework Knitters Petition* (1819), available via the House of Commons Parliamentary Papers website. Background information comes from Christopher Weir, *As Poor as a Stockinger* (2007), G. D. H. Cole and Raymond Postgate, *The Common People* (1946), Emma Griffin, *Liberty's Dawn* (2014), Robert Reid, *The Peterloo Massacre* (1989) and Brian Bailey, *The Luddite Rebellion* (1998).

19. The Workhouse
The words of the paupers in Andover Workhouse come from the Report of the Select Committee on Andover Union (1846). For background information see Ian Anstruther, *The Scandal of the Andover Workhouse* (1973), the *workhouses.org* website created by Ian Higginbotham, and M. A. Crowther, *The Workhouse System 1834-1929* (1981).

20. Immigrants

The words of the Irish immigrants in this chapter come from an article in the *Morning Chronicle* newspaper on 20 May 1850, entitled 'Labour and the Poor'. See also Lionel Rose, *Rogues and Vagabonds* (1988).

21. Street Orphans

The words of the flower girls and crossing-sweeper boys in this chapter are as recorded by Henry Mayhew in *London Labour and the London Poor*, vols 1 and 2 (1851).

22. The Casual Ward

This chapter is mainly based on James Greenwood's *A Night in a Workhouse* and Ellen Stanley's account in J. H. Stallard, *The Female Casual and her Lodging* (both from 1866). Charles Dickens' account of his visit to Wapping Workhouse in 1861 is in *The Uncommercial Traveller*. See also Henry Mayhew, *London Labour and the London Poor*, vol. 3 (1851), and *Pauper Capital: London and the Poor Law 1790-1870* (2010), by David R. Green. The opening scene is taken from the Luke Fildes painting 'Applicants for Admission to a Casual Ward', based on a print he made for *The Graphic* newspaper in 1869.

23. Sleeping Rough

The description of the homeless in St James' Park is drawn from a print in *The Graphic* newspaper of 1887. The speech and descriptions of the Embankment down-and-outs come from the account in William Booth, *In Darkest England* (1890). The scene in Trafalgar Square and the conversations of homeless there are adapted from articles by the journalist Howard Goldsmid in the *Hendon Courier* in October and November 1887, available online in the e-book *A Midnight Prowl Through Victorian London*.

Index

INDEX